COMMODORE VANDERBILT

by
Edwin P. Hoyt

REILLY & LEE CO., Chicago 1962

Illustrations reproduced through the courtesy
of the New York Historical Society

COPYRIGHT © 1962 BY EDWIN P. HOYT
MANUFACTURED IN THE UNITED STATES OF AMERICA
LIBRARY OF CONGRESS CARD NO. 62-16398

For Mother and Loye

CONTENTS

∽1∽

A BOY IN A
YOUNG REPUBLIC

Vanderbilt is an old name in American life. To most of
the people who grew up in the 1920's and 1930's the
name meant wealth and expensive living, huge parties
and ocean-going yachts, for that is how the Vanderbilts
of the twentieth century lived. They lived that way until
many of them had spent most of their fortunes. The
name Vanderbilt, in the 1940's and 1950's became a
symbol of waste to some, and to other people it recalled
glorious days of a past that would never be repeated in
America.

But the name Vanderbilt should not go down as a
symbol of waste and excessive luxury, for the real story
in the history of the Vanderbilt family is the story of a
boy who was born in George Washington's time, and
who grew up to become the richest man in the world.
His name was Cornelius Vanderbilt, or, in the beginning
of his life, Cornelius Van Derbilt. Both names are a
corruption of the words van der Bilt, which was not a
"name" at all, but a description.

Cornelius Vanderbilt's ancestors came to North
America a long time before the American Revolution.
The first of the line was a young man named Jan Aert-
son. He came to the New Netherlands colony of Nieuw

1

Nederland in 1640. A few years before Jan Aertson came, the Dutch East Indies Company had sent Henry Hudson on a trip to find a passage to India. Hudson had failed in his journey, but when he returned to Holland, this English sea captain told his Dutch employers the story of his voyage. They were particularly interested in his account of a voyage up a huge river on the American coastline, a river so deep that his sounding lines could scarce reach the bottom, with a current so swift that the lines were carried rapidly downstream, too.

The Dutch called this river the North River. Henry Hudson had sailed northward in his ship the *Half Moon* as far as what is now the city of Albany, New York. His report of the riches of the new land excited the Dutch burghers. He told of trading with the Indians for furs. He described the herds of game and the fish he had seen. And while he had failed to find a passage to the Far East, his story aroused so much interest in Holland that it was not long before a new trading company was formed to send traders and settlers to the new land.

Rich men formed that company—the Dutch West India Company. If other rich men would go to America and settle down they would be given large grants of land in the new country, on the condition that they would bring fifty settlers to the land and would help in the trade and colonization.

Jan Aertson became one of those hired settlers. He left his little village of Bilt, in the Dutch province of Utrecht, for the long, dangerous journey across the Atlantic ocean. When he arrived in Nieuw Nederland, he went ashore to the wooden stockade which had been built at the foot of Manhattan Island, in the center of the finest harbor men had ever seen on the North American continent. From there Jan Aertson was sent across the harbor to the house of Peter Wolpherson, one of the patroons who had come to the new land and had been given one of the huge estates. Jan Aertson agreed to become an indentured servant for three years, to pay for his passage on the ship and also for the few supplies and small bit of land he would need to start life again as an independent farmer.

All this happened in the year 1640. During the next three years Jan Aertson helped his patroon fight the Indians, who were growing warlike under the constant movement of the Dutch and English (in the north and east) against land the Indians had always owned. In those fights the women and children of the colony were shepherded down to the stockade at Fort Amsterdam, and the men patrolled the area or went on searching parties to drive out unfriendly bands of Indians. Many Indians and Dutchmen and women and children were killed in these wars, but finally the Indians realized that they could not win, and they retreated from the white settlements, or made peace and settled down to life with the whites.

At the end of this three years of service, Jan Aertson received a piece of land from the Wolphersons in the area of Flatbush in Breuckeleyn, just across the harbor from Manhattan. He built a house there, a house of logs and reeds and stones. He bought a plow and began to burn the stumps from his land and to haul the boulders and stones off to the sides for fences. He married, had children, and settled down to farming. Jan Aertson spoke Dutch, but before he died, Dutch was no longer the official language of the new colony. The English, who had come down from Massachusetts to Connecticut, and across from Connecticut to Long Island, began to crowd the Dutch. One day an English fleet invaded the harbor of New Amsterdam, and the commander demanded the surrender of the Dutch colony. The colony surrendered, and the British took possession in the name of the Duke of York. The name of the colony was changed to New York.

Dutch names were difficult for English settlers to understand, so it was not long before the Dutch names became changed. Jan Aertson's son, Aris, was known as Aris van der Bilt, a simple description which had appeared in Jan Aertson's papers to tell which Jan Aertson he was—from the village of Bilt. As time went on, the name was simplified, and soon it became Van Derbilt.

Aris Van der Bilt was as good a farmer as his father. He added to the land held by the family, and he bought more land in other areas. One piece of land he acquired was on the island off the Brooklyn shore—Staten Island. The Dutch bought Staten Island from the friendly Indians for ten shirts, thirty pairs of stockings, ten guns, thirty bars of lead, thirty pounds of powder, twelve coats, two pieces of luggage, thirty kettles, thirty hatchets, twenty hoes, and a case of nails and awls. That price shows what items were of value to both farmers and Indians in those days. Gold was valuable only for what it would buy in Europe. The Indians had no use for gold except to use it for jewelry or for ceremonial dresses and instruments. A hatchet was invaluable. So was a gun, and cloth was highly prized by the Indians who wore skins.

Brooklyn was a farming community in the seventeenth century, hardly a town at all. But it was becoming crowded at the end of the century. Seventeen hundred people and three hundred slaves (who were not regarded as people) lived in and around the Brooklyn area.

The son of Aris, a boy named Jacob, did not like the huge crowds around him in Brooklyn, so he took the wild land on Staten Island for his own, and when he married, he took his bride there to live in the wilderness.

At that time Staten Island was covered with dense scrub and underbrush, except in the salt meadows near the shore, and beneath the huge oaks and elms that towered above the land on the hills. Part of Jacob's land was clear meadow. He cleared the rest, keeping a good stand of timber to use for firewood for the rest of his life at least. He built a wooden house and all the buildings he would need for his farm, by ferrying every necessity from Brooklyn. There was no village on Staten Island. There was no store, no church, no meeting place, and no road. Only two hundred people lived on the island, and the van der Bilts were isolated from most of them. Jacob kept in touch with the outside world by using his boat, one of the fat, deep-bellied scows that the Dutch called *periaugers*. These periaugers had one or two masts and fore-and-aft sails which hung from gaff spars. They could not sail fast, but they could carry a great deal of cargo in the harbor, and that was the job they were built to do.

It was 1718 when Jacob Van der Bilt brought his new bride to the wild island to establish their home and farm. The French and the English were struggling for control of North America, but Jacob cared little for that. His life was a simple one, bounded by the shores of his island, for after he went to Staten Island to live, Jacob found little in common with his family which had remained on the mainland. Their ways of life were different. The rest of the family lived in what had become the luxury of towns and villages. Jacob and his growing family lived on the frontier. Everything they wanted cost effort.

In that first year, Jacob was busy building his house and barns, yet he planted a crop of corn and oats and such garden vegetables as they could save for the long winter. All the meat, fish, and other food had to be smoked or preserved for the cold months when travel was nearly impossible and hunting was difficult in the deep snow.

In 1719 Jacob Van der Bilt bought another hundred acres of land next to his own and set to work clearing that. Then he had as large a farm as he could work, and he settled down for good.

As time went on more people came to settle on Staten Island, and as the population increased, the people felt the need for churches and meeting-places. A group of Protestants from Europe made their way to America and to Staten Island. This group, known as the Moravians, who followed John Huss, built their mother church in Pennsylvania, but they left a strong settlement on Staten Island.

Within a few years, Jacob Van der Bilt had joined the church. Indeed, he was to become a lay brother in the church, and then an elder. He donated much money to send ships back to Europe to bring away the Moravians from central Europe, where they were being persecuted by their kings and the Catholic church for heresy.

Jacob Van der Bilt died in 1761 and left a large estate. But he also left a widow and eleven children to share it, so no share seemed very large to the next generation. The farm was sold at auction, and the proceeds were shared.

By this time, the Van der Bilt family had grown very

large. In Brooklyn, the family prospered and went into trade. One branch moved to Manhattan Island, where the name was changed to Vanderbilt. There Vanderbilts soon began to trade with the British West Indies and Britain in sugar and coffee and rum. But the Staten Island branch of the family was more old-fashioned, as islanders usually are. They were isolated from the rest, and they had not the advantages of education available in Manhattan and in Brooklyn. They lived lonely, withdrawn lives, as people on islands are inclined to do, too. Their greatest virtue was willingness to work hard.

One of the eleven children, young Jacob Van der Bilt, is the only one we are concerned with directly. He managed in a few years to create a farm about a quarter as large as that of his father. But six years after his father's death, young Jacob fell dead from his horse on the Courthouse Road, on a trip between the settlement and his fifty-acre farm. He, in turn, left seven children and a widow.

Since the children were young, it seemed foolish to break up the small estate. But the widow could not work the land herself, so it was rented out and she went to live with relatives, sending her children to live with other relatives. There was no government to support those who became old or sick. The families took care of themselves, and the way they did it was by "sharing out" the orphans and the widows, and taking turns in caring for aged mothers and fathers.

One of the children, Cornelius, was only a small child when his father Jacob died. He went to live with an uncle, and there he attended school for a few seasons. The school seasons were short, bounded in the spring by the planting season, when the youngsters could be put to work on the land, and by the cold snows of winter, which kept the youngsters of the farm families close to the hearth. Schooling did not seem very important on Staten Island then, and if it seemed important to some, there was little enough of it. The teacher usually was a part-time teacher who had just enough knowledge to handle a simple speller and reading book, and to teach the boys to cipher and to do simple sums. Some of the boys and girls learned history and philosophy from the Bible. They had almost no knowledge of current events, because there was no newspaper on Staten Island, as there were in New York and in Brooklyn, and there was very little concern with government or anything else except farming, fishing, and trade.

Cornelius was educated in a different school. He learned to milk cows, tend pigs, sheep, and horses. He learned to sail a boat and to plow. He learned how to build a haystack that would not mildew and rot. He learned quickness and obedience and the use of his eyes and ears. He became a boatman and ferried loads of cabbages, onions, and turnips to the New York and Brooklyn markets in the summer. In the winter, he tended the woodpile, cut trees for lumber, and helped with the horses. He dressed in homespun shirts and trousers. His boots were made of oxhide. He seldom wore underclothes of any kind, and then only to keep warm. Nor did he wear stockings except in the coldest part of winter.

This Cornelius was quick enough of brain, and he never could fully accept the drudgery of the farm life. He had never wanted to be a farmer, but circumstances had made him a farmer and a boatman.

Eight years after his father died, the American Revolution began. The Revolution did not directly affect Staten Island too much, except that British and Hessian troops were quartered there. It was wisest for women and children to stay inside at night. Men, too, stayed at home nights, because they were afraid of being accused by the British of spying for the Revolutionaries, or being accused by the Revolutionaries who raided the island of working for the British.

But what did happen in those Revolutionary years to the Staten Islanders? The most important thing that happened was that they were isolated, as no other part of America had been, by the continued presence of British forces all through the war. They were out of touch with all that was American. George Washington was so enraged by the attitude of some Staten Islanders that he declared all of them were Tories. This was not true. Most of them were just not interested in the war, because they were Dutch who had never been truly brought into the British colonial way of thinking, and because they were quiet islanders.

New York—Manhattan Island—was held by the British, too, but New York had a different history during the war. Most of the people who stayed there during the war were British sympathizers. They hoped for an early end to the rebellion and felt confident that once the rebellion was crushed, life would go on as it had before. In New Jersey, in upper New York colony, and in the rest of the colonies outside British occupation territory, most of the people supported the Revolution. But the Staten Islanders lived in occupied territory, and they were to suffer from both sides during the war.

Cornelius Van der Bilt worked on the farm in those years. It did not seem to occur to him to run away and join the Revolutionaries. Some of his cousins from Brooklyn fought for the Revolution, but practically no one on Staten Island did, and Cornelius was not aroused.

The war ended in 1783, after the British Parliament refused to continue fighting. General George Washington had captured Lord Cornwallis' entire army of eight thousand men at Yorktown in 1781. In that same year and in 1782 the French, allied with the Americans, had defeated the British in the West Indies, and the House of Commons voted to end the war. A treaty was arranged in negotiations at Paris, and in the fall of 1783, the British garrisons of New York and Staten Island sailed for home, taking with them twelve thousand Tories who did not want to remain on American soil.

Four years later, Cornelius Van der Bilt was a grown man. He kept a small farm near the Kill Van Kull, a narrow waterway which separates Staten Island from the shore of New Jersey. He did not own the land, but rented it. He did not own any land, because the Revolution had cost Cornelius his share of the estate of his father. During the war, the Revolutionary Americans had sneaked ashore one night and burned the courthouse on Staten Island, destroying all the records. Thus, after the war, it was almost impossible for the authorities to settle the many property arguments and claims. In the arguments, Cornelius lost whatever property he might have been entitled to. Cornelius did have a horse or two of his own, and he owned a periauger now, in which he hauled produce, grain, and hay for other farmers and brought back supplies from the mainland.

One day, after he had finished his work on the water, he rode to the house of the Reverend Mr. Johnson, one of the few ministers on the island. There he encountered Mr. Johnson's sister-in-law, a young girl named Phebe Hand, who had come from New Jersey to live with her sister. They fell in love. That year they were married, and Phebe Hand moved into the rude cottage on the Kill Van Kull to begin to raise a family.

Of their children—and there were to be nine of them —the first son died at an early age. Only two daughters survived, but before the first son (Jacob) died, he had been joined by a brother named Cornelius—the Vanderbilt who was to become the richest man in the world.

But there were no signs in the spring of 1794 that the son of this stolid Dutch couple would become the most powerful man in America. The family outgrew its cottage and moved to a house in Stapleton, farther east on Staten Island, not long after young Cornelius was born. To differentiate between father and son, the family called the boy Corneel. Corneel grew up to look much like his father, who was a handsome man. The boy was blond, tall, and spare. He was to grow eventually to be more than six feet tall (at a time when the average American was less than five feet nine inches tall) and he was to become strong and sturdy as an ox.

Corneel had even less schooling than his father, because he hated school. He liked working with the animals. When he was about six years old he raced one of his father's plow horses against that of another boy aged eight. Corneel won the race, although the horse was not made for that kind of work.

Before he was ten years old, Corneel quit school. It was the year of his elder brother's death, and the family did not object too seriously, because the boy was needed now to help his father with the regular ferry service the elder Cornelius ran between Staten Island and Manhattan.

Every morning in the clement months, the sound of a conch horn at Van Derbilt's landing heralded the imminent departure of the elder Cornelius' ferry for the mainland. It was not much of a vessel—a two-masted periauger—but it was the best service Staten Island had to offer. An occasional businessman made his way to the

wharf to line up with farmers carrying pigs in a wheel-
barrow, or bringing a load of hay to be stuffed in the
hold or a wagon full of cabbages to send their earthy smell
through the boat as she ponderously made her way across
the blue-green water of New York harbor. Clutching his
hat tightly to his breast, the unfortunate businessman
might pile aboard the periauger, atop the load of hay,
cabbages, and pigs, crushed in with strong-smelling
farmers and their pipe-smoking wives, who might be going to the city to buy a bit of cotton or a few pots to
replace those worn out since the last visit of the peddling
costermonger.

It was not a long voyage. It might be made in less than
two hours if the wind was fair, even with a full load under
the heavy lug sails. But usually the wind stood foul for
home, and that meant beating a way back and forth
across the channel, heading for Brooklyn perhaps, and
then cutting sharply back again to take advantage of
the wind, or in the last resort, poling the heavy scow
with the long oaken sticks that were so heavy it was
hard to believe a ten-year-old could handle one of them.

These were busy years for young Van Derbilt, just as
they were busy years for a nation fighting pirates in
Tripoli and buying the Louisiana Purchase territory.
Thomas Jefferson was the President of the United States.
Washington, who had been President when Corneel was
born, had been dead for five years. Lewis and Clark had
set forth on their remarkable expedition to the far western reaches of the continent. Aaron Burr and Alexander
Hamilton dueled that year, ending a quarrel that had
dragged on for years—but ending it in the most tragic
possible way for both, with the death of Hamilton and
the exile and disgrace of the talented Burr.

Such matters had little interest for the Van Derbilts

of Staten Island. One must remember how low they were on the social scale of the American Republic to gather how little it meant to any of them that Hamilton was dead, that Jefferson was worried about the tiny nation's future, or that a treacherous attempt at establishment of a Northern confederacy (the Essex Junto) was being plotted in the drawing rooms of some Massachusetts citizens.

None of the Van Derbilts would have known what the inside of a drawing room looked like. They would have been insensible to the difference between a glass of vintage wine and a pot of the rotgut sold in taverns. They were more used to the straight spirit or straight gin that was the common drink. They were not comfortable using knives and forks in the gentlemanly fashion. Indeed, to understand the family, one must recall that they were only a few generations removed from serfdom, and that those generations in America had been spent in the rude huts of the frontier, where the hunting knife had many uses—not least of which was as principal utensil for eating.

The ladies and gentlemen of New York, such as John Jay, the Roosevelts, and the Van Rennselaers, dressed in silks and satins. The men wore worsted knee breeches with buckles at the knee and on their polished shoes. Their linen was ruffled and clean, and they powdered their hair and scented their faces.

The Van Derbilts and the other Staten Islanders still wore homespun and rude shoes of coarse leather. Their cloth clothing consisted of the cheapest cottons and inferior woollens which were the best they could afford. But they were far better off, as farmers, than the poverty-stricken city dwellers who worked in the frightful, sickening tannery of the Roosevelts behind the city front, or who labored in the slaughterhouses or the shipyards. The workers' homes in New York were poor enough, but the homes of the very poor were dirt-floored hovels, without plumbing or any conveniences whatsoever. Nor were the poor so careful as to use outhouses. They threw their slops in the streets, bringing rats, flies, and filth to their very doorsteps.

So, poor as they were and rude as they might be by other standards, the Van Derbilts were not to be pitied. They lived healthful lives, and they were as well off as most farmers in the area. Father Cornelius had gathered together enough money, through the saving habits of his wife, to buy a farm to adjoin his house at Stapleton. He owned his own scow. He prospered, according to weather and the seasons, but he did not go into debt and thus was never faced with the awful prospect of debtor's prison —in which a man sat in a cell, unable to secure freedom until his debt was paid, and unable to get out and work to pay the debt.

In those years of boyhood, Corneel Van Derbilt did a man's work. Once in a while he had time for gaiety, but not often, and even then there was usually a bit of work attached before the boyish fun could begin.

For example, one day when he was about twelve years old, Corneel secured his father's permission to borrow the periauger for a boy's trip to New York. He and another youth had planned to spend an entire day in the city, wandering up and down the crooked streets, looking inside the fish markets, meat markets, and clothing stores, perhaps even spending a penny or two on sweets. It was to be real adventure. Old Cornelius had made the promise in an offhand way, but he had given his word, so Corneel was sure he would have the boat. Early in the morning of the day in question Corneel and his friend went to the wharf, only to see his father slowly pitching a load of hay into the bottom of the periauger.

Corneel's heart fell. He was sure his father had forgotten. But the elder Van Derbilt casually tossed the hay fork to his son and told him he could pitch in the rest, deliver the hay, and then they could have the rest of the day for their excursion.

Other days, Corneel did even harder work. As the Van Derbilt skill with boats became known around the island, father and son were called upon to do many tasks. On one occasion, when Corneel was in his early teens, his father was asked to handle the problem of a ship which had gone ashore on the sands at Sandy Hook in the lower harbor, on the New Jersey coast. The old man decided that he would handle the lighters, the shallow-draft boats which would carry the cargo from the ship to the docks. But somebody had to go by land to the grounded ship, with horses and wagons to get the cargo into the lighters. Corneel was trustworthy enough that his father chose him to do the job and to command a force of men and several teams of horses.

Corneel made his way by ferry and by road down to the New Jersey coast and to Sandy Hook. The job was begun early that morning and it was late that night before the weary crews began the long trip home. Corneel's father had given him just enough money to pay the ferry tolls. Nothing had been said about meals. The men had brought their lunches, but the day had been long, and work had gone on past their usual supper hour. They were tired. They wanted a hot meal and a drink before they started home.

As they passed through a town, Corneel made his decision. He stopped at a tavern and bought the men a meal. He paid the bill, but then had nothing left with which to pay the ferryman for taking them across the Kill Van Kull. When Corneel arrived at the ferry, he reached an impasse. The ferryman would not take them without money, and, of course, they could get no money until Corneel went home for some.

Finally, Corneel made an arrangement with the ferryman. He left one horse on the ferry. If he did not return within two days, he said, the ferryman could sell the horse and keep the difference as profit. The ferryman agreed, and the party went home.

When Corneel arrived at home, his father was furious. He accused the boy of having thought more of his stomach than of his work. Corneel said nothing but he determined, right then, that he would get out from under his parents' rule and go into business for himself as soon as he could manage it.

~2~

THE SAILOR

FOR AS LONG as he could remember, Corneel had hated working in the fields of his father's Staten Island farm. After his elder brother Jacob died, and Corneel left the tiny school, he had hoed onions in the spring and summer, harvested the cabbages, and helped his father just as a grown hired man might have.

The one part of farm life Corneel liked was work with the horses, sturdy plow nags though they were. Astride the broad back of one of the work horses, he could dream that he was racing or riding off to adventure away from the drudgery of the farm. The horses and the work on the family ferry were the enjoyable parts of Corneel's life.

As he contemplated his future, the youngster realized that the sea offered him an escape, and perhaps his only escape, from stolid farm life. There was no future in horses for him, but there might be a future in boats. That there was no future in working with his father, either, Corneel learned before he was sixteen years old.

One day the boy suggested that instead of ferrying between Staten Island and Whitehall Slip at the foot of Manhattan, he and his father should roam the harbor,

17

looking for freight to haul. But such an idea was beyond the comprehension of the elder Vanderbilt. He brushed it aside roughly. Still, Corneel did not forget the idea. He found the ordinary Staten Island boatmen a lazy lot. They sailed out from the island to Manhattan early in the morning, then sat at the foot of Whitehall and smoked their pipes and gossiped until someone came along with a hauling job to be done. They might sit there all day, wasting time Corneel thought, when they could be out on the harbor earning money. There was no shortage of work. New York was growing rapidly. Ships came into the deep port from all over the world, and cargoes were sitting on the dockside, waiting to be moved to Brooklyn, to New Jersey, and to Long Island.

Before Corneel was seventeen years old he felt ready for a life of his own. One day he traveled across the harbor to Manhattan and went in search of it, moving in and out of the lanes of ocean-going ships pulled up against the docks. At last he found what he wanted, a ship that would soon be pulling out of port, bound for the high seas and Atlantic adventure. Corneel found the captain of the ship and signed on as apprentice hand. He was determined to escape the drudgery of the farm.

That night, Corneel went home and confided his plans to his mother. He poured out his story of mistreatment and disagreement with his father. He told Phebe Hand that he was determined to escape the life of a farmer. His mother could see from the set of that solid jaw, so much like her own, that Corneel meant what he said. She promised that she would do what she could to help him change his lot, if he would agree not to go to sea but to stay at home with the family.

Corneel knew why his mother wanted him to stay at home. There was danger in shipping out before the mast

as a hand, but it was not that. In those days of the early
nineteenth century, there was a serious labor shortage
in America. The land was vast, the people few. Because
there were so few people in the entire country, the labor
of a young man belonged to his family until he reached
his majority or until he married and started a family of
his own.

Phebe Hand Vanderbilt did not want Corneel to go to
sea because the family needed every bit of help he could
give them. Her husband, of course, wanted Corneel to
stay on the Staten Island farm, but she knew this was no
longer possible, so she found her own way of resolving
the problem. Corneel agreed to stay home and not ship
out, but only for a time, and only if he could achieve his
independence.

Just before Corneel's seventeenth birthday, he came
to his mother with a specific plan. He knew of a periauger
that was for sale. He wanted to buy it and go into the
hauling business for himself. The problem was that the
periauger cost a hundred dollars. Corneel, who gave
everything he earned to the family, did not have a single
dollar of his own. Would his mother help him, he asked?

Phebe Hand was a stern woman and sometimes she
was harsh. To survive in that age a woman had to be
stern, especially if she was trying to raise eight children
on a tiny, rocky island farm. Still, Phebe Hand loved her
son. She said she would help him in her own way, and she
went to the grandfather's clock that stood on the kitchen
floor to prove her intention.

That grandfather's clock had stood on the kitchen floor
of the Vanderbilt house for as long as Corneel could
remember. It had traveled with them from the first tiny
cottage on the Kill Van Kull to the new, bigger Dutch
house at Stapleton, the new two story white house with

its tall sentinel chimneys at each end. The clock was Phebe Hand's bank, and hers alone. No one else in the family ever dared go into it, but there Phebe Hand kept the money the family saved, dollar by dollar.

How much was in the clock?

No one in the family knew that secret, but Corneel did know that one time, when his father had come home discouraged because he had no money to pay off a mortgage, his mother had reached into her clock and pulled forth three thousand dollars.

On this spring day, Phebe Hand went into her clock once again, then thought better of it. If Corneel wanted a hundred dollars, she said, he could earn a loan from her.

And what would he have to do?

It was the first day of May, 1810. If Corneel would plow and plant the corn in the eight-acre plot behind the house, before his birthday on May 27, Phebe would lend him the hundred dollars he wanted to buy his boat.

Eight acres in twenty-seven days. It seemed impossible, but Corneel took on the job. It *was* impossible for a sixteen year old boy, with one horse and a single blade plow, to do this job by himself. But Corneel made no attempt to do it by himself. Instead, he enlisted the help of neighbor boys, promising them fishing trips and sailing excursions in his periauger once the job was done.

When May 27 arrived, the job was finished and Corneel went proudly to his mother to collect the hundred dollars he had earned. Then he went off across the island to buy his boat. He was going into business for himself.

In a few days Corneel began to earn money with the periauger. New York City was growing into the most important port in the new American republic. As New York grew, so did the little villages around her, villages like Brooklyn and Newark. Other ports up and down this part of the Atlantic shore also grew. In New Jersey, for a time, the towns of Elizabeth and New Brunswick vied with New York for the trade of the farmers inland. They never could compete with the big trading companies which sprang up at the foot of Manhattan Island, but the two towns did have much trade and much to be hauled by busy boatmen.

Nor were the port towns of New Jersey and New York Harbor the only places where a boatman could profit. Up the Hudson River, towns were scattered along both banks. In these days, when roads were muddy tracks and the railroad had not yet come to America, the basic means of transportation was by boat. Most of the towns in this new America were located on rivers or on good harbors, and the big cities were located seaward of the fall line, that point at which rivers become too shallow for ocean-going ships to navigate.

Corneel agreed, as part of the price of receiving his freedom from the farm, that he would turn his earnings over to the family. That was only fair. If Corneel did not want to work on the farm or on the family ferry, his father had to hire a man to help until young Jacob Hand Vanderbilt, the only other living boy in the family, could be of some use. Jacob Hand Vanderbilt in 1810 was only three years old—not even old enough to pull weeds out of the onion patch.

Other seventeen-year-olds liked to amuse themselves after their day's work was done, but not Corneel Vanderbilt. His work was never done. He arose at dawn, crept down the ladder from the loft above the big common room of the house, and hurried outside to his boat. He unfurled the sails, hoisted the gaff spar up the tall mast, and set out for the day's adventure, either traveling through the upper bay toward the Hudson, or down the Kill Van Kull or through the Narrows to the lower bay. At night, when the other youths and the country girls wanted amusement, they traveled across the harbor from Staten Island to Manhattan, where they might visit Fraunces Tavern, that famous gathering place where Washington had said goodbye to his troops a few years before. Or, they might go to a traveling minstrel show. Or perhaps some magician or some traveling troupe would be performing at one of the local theaters.

Corneel Vanderbilt never wasted his time or his money on entertainment in those ways. He was the boatman who was always ready to take the others across the harbor, and to wait for them during the night hours. He slept while they amused themselves, and he was paid even while he was sleeping.

The next morning, when the others arose tired and irritable from their night of gaiety, Corneel Vanderbilt was already out on the water, earning money once again.

He was not the only able boatman or the only ambitious man on Staten Island. For years the Vanderbilt had been competing in the ferry trade with their neighbors, the Van Duzers. Like the Vanderbilts, the Van Duzers owned a large periauger to haul vegetables across the bay, but unlike the Vanderbilts, the Van Duzers had never kept a regular schedule. Jake Van Duzer, who was Corneel's age and was also Corneel's greatest rival, always tried to win his victories by strength and shrewdness.

One day when Corneel was carrying some passengers over to Brooklyn in his periauger, he became involved in a contest with Jake Van Duzer, who boasted that his periauger was faster than Vanderbilt's and that he was also a better boatman.

It was a warm summer day. Corneel was poling his boat through Buttermilk Channel, which runs between Governors Island and the Brooklyn docks. The air that day was almost still and the sails were nearly useless. It was manpower, not windpower, that moved boats swiftly across the harbor that day.

Corneel was lost in his own thoughts, lulled by the regular physical motion of the poling. Back and forth he poled, his brown arms and strong back gleaming and moving rhythmically in the bright sunshine.

He did not notice that another periauger was creeping up on him, until the shadow of the mast cut across his boat. Then he turned to see Jake Van Duzer, grinning like an idiot, poling past him as quickly as he could move his boat. It was to be a race. That much was obvious. It might not be so obvious to the passengers that the superiority of Corneel as Staten Island's best boatman was being challenged, but that was the truth. Corneel, had he been wide awake, would never have allowed Jake Van Duzer to come so close.

Corneel was now at a disadvantage. Jake Van Duzer had built up a great deal of momentum in the poling that brought him alongside, and now he slid quickly ahead. Corneel, starting from slow motion, had to bring his periauger to the same speed, or lose the race hopelessly before it was well begun.

A frown creased Corneel's brown face as the young man began to push on the pole with all his strength. The veins stood out in his neck as he poled along. His heart pounded and the sweat beaded his forehead in the hot sun. He went faster, faster, and faster. Would he ever catch up to the puffing, larger Van Duzer, who had gained such a head start on him? He could not take time out to look, except to cast a sidelong glance across the water. Any break in his rhythm and the race would be lost to Van Duzer.

Corneel poled and pushed harder than ever before in his life. Finally he saw Van Duzer's boat alongside, and he poled even harder, until his boat struck the bank with a bump, jolting his passengers. By less than a length, he won the race that day.

Even while he won, Corneel gained a memento he was never to lose. The immense effort of poling the periauger almost from a standstill to racing speed had cost him dear. The end of the pole had torn a hole in his flesh, just at the breastbone. He was to carry the scar for the rest of his life, a reminder of his early proud efforts to be first in his own field.

For a time during that first summer, Corneel spent many hours hauling passengers. The fare from Whitehall to Staten Island was eighteen cents. With twenty or thirty passengers in a periauger, a boatman could earn between three and six dollars, a very fair day's wage, it seemed.

The trouble was that most boatmen were satisfied with that one trip to earn their day's wages, and if they picked up a return fare of half the size, they were well pleased indeed. Most of them failed to think of the many winter and gusty spring days when their boats were laid up in harbor, and of the expense of buying the boat and keeping it in sailing condition.

Corneel learned quickly that while the passenger trade seemed to be lucrative, there were much better ways of making money on the harbor. Hauling freight was one way, for if he did a good job of hauling freight, he could count on return business from the same merchants and farmers. He could also work in his own way, and at his own pace, and schedule his own work so as to make it easiest and most profitable for him. So Corneel concentrated on freight hauling. He carried bags of grain, hay, and straw in the periauger from the island to the city across the harbor. He carried barrels of tar, molasses, and pickles to the market place. He took on cows and swine and anything that would bring a profit. He earned good profits, too. Before that first summer as a boatman was ended he had paid Phebe Hand back the hundred dollars he had borrowed to buy his boat, and at the end of the year he had contributed a thousand dollars to the family income.

The next year, 1811, Corneel earned even more money. He saved five hundred dollars of his own that year, besides contributing to the family. He bought a new periauger, the largest on the island. He painted her black, and he called her *Dread,* to show the other boatman that he was the man to be respected and feared in the Staten Island hauling trade. *Dread* was a very large boat. She measured sixty-two feet from stem to stern and was almost half that wide. It took at least two men to sail her and care for the cargo, but Corneel was now in business for himself, and with his new boat he could afford to hire other men to help him. He also bought shares in two other periaugers.

But even while Corneel was laying the basis for a successful business, world events were changing the life around him.

Great Britain ruled the seas in those days, and British ships needed many seamen. Sometimes British sailors deserted in foreign ports, and sometimes after they had deserted, they joined the crews of American ships. The British soon discovered this practice, and often stopped American ships to search for deserters from the navy.

Sometimes they found them, and sometimes, if a ship needed men, they forced Americans to join the crews of warships.

On June 18, 1812, the American government declared war on Great Britain.

This war did not change Corneel Vanderbilt's life very much, although it put some new restrictions on his work. No longer was it safe to take the *Dread* into the lower bay, because blockading British warships stood off the Narrows and off Navesink on the New Jersey coast, ready to stop and seize any ship or even large boat and the crew that was so foolhardy as to bring the boat into open water.

Corneel's business did not end, however. And to make up for the loss of the lower bay trade, he found new business in the port itself, where provisions were short, and it was necessary to supply the growing, crowded city of New York from the water. Also, as the Americans prepared for a British attack they feared, they sent troops into the city and to man the forts that protected the harbor from the sea. Those soldiers needed supplies, and they had to move back and forth across the harbor by boat. So there was plenty of work for Corneel and the other boatmen, even during the worst years of the war.

There were, however, fewer boatmen. When war was declared, the United States Navy was so tiny it could not hope to wage effective warfare against the huge British fleet. It was true that the British were far more concerned about the danger to them in Europe, where they were warring with Napoleon's French armies. Still a single squadron of British ships was more than enough to bottle up New York, and the Americans, with a few ships like the USS *Constitution* and the USS *Constellation*, had very little with which to fight. So the American Navy commissioned a great number of *privateers*. These were stout merchant ships which were fitted with guns and fighting crews. They tried to sneak out of the American harbors under the eyes of the British. If they were successful, they would head south, toward the British West Indies, to prey on British merchant ships.

There was much money to be made in a successful privateering venture, even for crewmen. But it was neither so glamorous nor so profitable a venture as many of these seamen believed, for the real profits went to the captains and the owners of the privateers. The seamen risked their necks for glory and good pay—but the pay was not enough to make their fortunes, even if they were successful.

Corneel Vanderbilt gave little thought to privateering. He was interested in building for the future, not in joining the navy or in taking a long chance to make profit. He continued to haul passengers and freight in the *Dread* and his other boats.

Corneel had proved himself at nineteen to be the best boatman on the New York Harbor. One day in October, 1813, the people and the army officers in New York heard a rumor that the British would try to attack the city. All New York was fearful that this might happen, because the people remembered the Revolutionary War, when the British landed troops on Staten Island and on Long Island, and then descended on New York and captured it after defeating General Washington's force. This time, the people feared that the British might try to run through the channel between Staten Island and Brooklyn and capture the port from the inside.

That channel was protected by Fort Richmond, which stood high above the water on Staten Island. The fort's guns could fire into any ship that tried to pass through the channel. But if enough ships came through, and if the wind was right, the fort could not hope to sink them all. It would take only two or three ships of the line to wreak havoc in New York, and perhaps even to capture the city if the ships were able to move inside the defenses.

Before the telegraph was invented, in bad weather the only way news could be sent from Staten Island to New York was by messenger. On that fall day, although a storm was blowing, the commander of Fort Richmond was so sure an attempt would be made to run the channel that he ordered the fires heated, and the cannon balls made red hot to burn their way through the sides of the ships if they should try to attack.

There was no attack, but the storm was so great the people of New York had no way of knowing what had happened. The only way the commander could ease their minds was to send messengers across the stormy harbor.

In the face of the howling wind and the huge waves that splashed high on the shore only the best boatman on the island could hope to get across safely, carrying officers who would bring the word to the army commanders in New York. So the garrison commander called for the best boatman of all, and the Staten Islanders brought forth Corneel Vanderbilt to do the job.

"Can you make the trip?" the commander asked.

Corneel looked out at the heaving green seas, which were sure to break over the bows of his periauger. "Yes," he said. "But I shall have to carry the men under the water part of the way."

And Corneel did just that.

Few men questioned Corneel Vanderbilt's bravery, although he had no desire to join the navy or to fight, either with a gun or with his fists. He was interested most of all in making his own fortune, but he realized that if he was to do so he must build a reputation for honesty and hard work.

One day during the war, Corneel's nature was sorely provoked. He was carrying a load of soldiers from Fort Richmond to New York. As they passed the quarantine station on Staten Island, another boat pulled out and swiftly moved alongside Corneel's heavily laden periauger. This boat bore only its master, a competitor of Corneel's, and a pompous lieutenant in the army. The lieutenant cupped his hands and shouted to Corneel to pull into the quarantine station for inspection. Corneel knew there was no good reason for this command. The quarantine had been established to keep check on strangers, who might have diseases such as typhoid fever and cholera. These soldiers were coming straight from Fort Richmond. There was no reason for them to stop at quarantine. Corneel suspected that it was a trick to take the soldiers off his boat and put them on the boat of his competitor, who seemed to be friendly with the officer.

Corneel refused to turn the boat around or to stop. The other boatman brought his empty boat alongside, and the officer leaped aboard Corneel's periauger. Then he commanded Corneel to turn around and began to draw his sword in threat. Corneel stood up, drew back his fist, hit the officer, and knocked him down. Then he dumped him over the side into the other boat. After that he continued on his way to Whitehall Slip to deliver his passengers to New York.

Corneel never heard another word about that incident.

Most of the time Corneel's relations with the army were good. He hauled hay for the horses and provisions for the troops from the "market garden" of Staten Island to the city. In the spring of 1814, he also was given a contract that made him the most important boatman in all New York Harbor, not just on Staten Island.

The war was still in progress and New York was suffering. While some merchant ships managed to run the blockade the British had thrown up around the port, the city was filled with frightened people. Every month or two a new rumor was spread about an imminent invasion by the British. The citizens and the soldiers threw up earthworks along the East River and along the Hudson River. That spring, Governor Daniel Tompkins called up the militia of the state to serve for three months because he was afraid the British would try to attack the city during the summer.

When the militia was called, it meant that every ablebodied man who could be spared from important work was to go to the defense of the state. Rich men might find excuses, but the poor and the workingmen could seldom get out of service.

For that reason, the call for the militia worried all the boatmen in New York Harbor. It meant they would have to give up their work during the most profitable time of the year and serve as common soldiers.

One way to get out of the service was to find a contract with the government. With the call for the militia to increase the garrisons of the six forts that encircled New York Harbor more provisions would be needed, so a new contract was offered. All the boatmen began to prepare their bids, and all but one of them made the bids very low because they would rather not make any profits if they could just stay out of service.

Corneel Vanderbilt was the one boatman who refused to cut his price. He said that if the work was worth doing it was worth doing well—and for a fair price. The Commissary General of the American forces, General Matthew

Davis, agreed with Vanderbilt. The general was annoyed by the boatmen who were trying to stay out of the service of their state in a time of war. So General Davis awarded the contract to Corneel Vanderbilt.

That contract was a real step forward for Corneel. Not only did it mean a good profit, but in the way he managed his affairs it did not even interfere with his normal working day. He decided to supply the forts at night—traveling to a different fort each night of the week. The provisions were made ready and placed on the wharf at six o'clock every evening. After a full day of work in the harbor, Corneel sailed up to the New York dock, took the provisions aboard, and sailed for one of the forts. He supplied Fort Washington, Fort Lee, and Governors Island, which lies between New York and Staten Island. He supplied the other forts each week, too, with guns, bullets, powder, and food and clothing for the troops.

When the war ended, Corneel Vanderbilt was just twenty-one years old, but he now had enough money to engage in shipping on a greater scale. He bought a schooner from the federal government, which was cutting down the size of its navy, and he sailed south to Virginia on his first long voyage. A few months later, in the summer of 1815, Corneel went into partnership with his brother-in-law, Captain John DeForest. They built a schooner which they called the *Charlotte* in honor of DeForest's wife, Corneel's sister. Now that the war was over, there was an immediate and huge demand for all the important goods that could not be brought in through the British blockade. The people of the cities needed oil for their lamps and cotton and woollen goods. They wanted wine, spirits, and spices. Once the war ended it was simple enough for the businessmen to bring the goods into the ports of New York, Boston, and Baltimore. But the big ships found it hard sailing up the narrow, twisting rivers where so many cities and towns had grown up. So there was all the business anyone could want for the men who were foresighted enough to go into the coastal trade. Corneel and DeForest prospered in that first year—enough so that they were soon investing in other vessels.

Corneel found, however, that he preferred to let DeForest handle the schooner and the coastal end of the business, while he remained in New York harbor. There was more money to be made there.

He had another reason for wanting to stay home. Two years before, when Corneel was nineteen years old, he had decided to get married. At first his mother and father objected. They said he was too young to begin raising a family; besides, the girl he wanted to marry—Sophia Johnson—was his first cousin. But Corneel almost always got his own way. He could prove that he was responsible, because for two years he had been contributing heavily to the support of the family. He brushed aside the objection to his blood relationship with Sophia. He simply ignored that argument. So he and Sophia were married in 1813, and they went for a time to live with Corneel's family in the white Dutch cottage at Stapleton. Corneel seemed to be settling down to become a Staten Island shipping man.

～3～

THE YOUNG CAPTAIN

ONCE THE WAR of 1812 ended, Corneel Vanderbilt found opportunity in the whole of New York Harbor once again. Then, as now, the harbor was a vast stretch of protected water, lying at the point of a large angle. One arm of the angle is the south shore of Long Island, which stretches 104 miles from Coney Island to Montauk Point. The other arm runs south along the New Jersey coast for a hundred miles, from Sandy Hook to Cape May.

In between there was and is little that is larger than a cove into which a schooner could dart to protect itself from the weather or to unload cargo. And in 1815 the whole area was growing rapidly in population. By the end of the war, New York City was the greatest commercial center in America. A hundred thousand people lived in the city itself in some sixteen thousand homes. There were thirteen hundred grocery stores and a hundred and sixty taverns. The city awoke late, since business did not begin before nine o'clock, but it stayed up late, too, using whale oil lamps for lighting.

All this took transport, and transport meant the type of boat Corneel Vanderbilt was running. There was business to be done in unloading the bigger ships near the Jersey shore, if their cargo was to go south. There was business in salvage, too, after ocean-going ships went aground in storms on the sandy coast of New Jersey, or on spike-toothed reefs offshore.

One November day in 1817 the captain and owners of a ship named the *Neptune* found Captain Vanderbilt aboard the *Dread* at the Vanderbilt landing and asked for his help. The weather was rough, so rough that the *Neptune* had run aground on the beach at Sandy Hook, the captain said. And even though the weather was foul, there was no time to be lost in salvaging the cargo.

What cargo could be so valuable, Vanderbilt asked.

Four hundred and six thousand dollars in gold, the captain replied. If they did not get it off the ship before the storm broke again, the *Neptune* might break to pieces, and the gold would be lost forever in the shifting sands.

Corneel did not hesitate. He drove a hard bargain for profit, and well he might, for it was a dangerous job in which he risked his *Dread* and his own life. Not then, or ever after, did Corneel Vanderbilt take out insurance on his ships. He preferred to run the risk and use the money he would otherwise have paid for insurance to build his fortune.

Luck was with him, as it usually seemed to be. Corneel and the crew of the *Dread* rescued the gold and were well paid for their trouble. Another risk had paid off.

In a few years after the war Corneel became one of the best-known sailing captains in the harbor area, famed because he would undertake any job, and once the bargain was made, he would stick to it through all kinds of adversity. Yet primarily Corneel was not an adventurer but a businessman. Most of his work was plain, hard hauling, with little romance to it.

In one town Vanderbilt became famous for his business methods. He had often come to this town before—to New

Brunswick, New Jersey—but on one occasion he made his reputation.

It was springtime, when the shad run up the Delaware, the Hudson, and the other rivers of the central states of the Atlantic coast. Shad provided an important part of the diet of the farmers and townspeople in those days, for like the salmon of the west coast, the silvery shad run in huge schools, leaping obstacles and threading narrow raceways in their drive to reach the fresh water where they were spawned.

Always in the past the farmers of New Brunswick and all of central New Jersey had purchased their shad from fishermen on the Delaware and the southern rivers. Their whole orientation was south, toward Philadelphia and Chesapeake Bay. The farmers bought their fish by the barrel, then brought them home to pickle them in brine and stow them away in the spring house or cold cellar to keep through the summer and into winter.

Vanderbilt could see no reason why all the shad trade should go to the southern fishermen and boatmen, particularly since he had business to do in New Brunswick from time to time and hated to sail down there from Staten Island with an empty boat.

So one day Corneel loaded his periauger to the gunwales with fresh shad from the Hudson River, and set sail for the Raritan on the New Jersey coast, then sailed up the Raritan to New Brunswick.

Captain Vanderbilt had thirty thousand shimmering shad on the periauger that day, and absolutely no assurance that the people of New Jersey would buy them. It was a very risky venture.

When he reached New Brunswick and tied up at the wharf at the foot of Burnet Street, Vanderbilt must have felt his worst nightmares had come true. The people of

New Brunswick were not interested in Hudson River shad. They had no assurance that they were fresh. The whole idea of buying from the Hudson River was new, and all the fish markets, provender stores, and street hawkers resisted it.

So what was Corneel to do? He was sitting at the dock with thirty thousand fish on his hands, a perishable cargo that must be disposed of within twenty-four hours if it was to be worth anything at all.

Vanderbilt had come to New Brunswick with a plan to be executed in just such an emergency. He hired five horsemen to ride out into the countryside, along the roads to Flemington, Princeton, and Freehold, announceing all the way that there was fresh shad down at New Brunswick to be had at less than the market price—better shad than usual, for these were Hudson River shad.

The new sales approach worked. Farmers and townspeople flocked to Burnet Street to buy directly from the boat. Vanderbilt sold out his load of fish at a handsome profit, and when he was finished with his other business and returned to New Brunswick again a few days later, he brought another load.

Corneel was making a good living as a schooner captain and from his periauger hauling trade, but something happened that same year that set him to thinking hard about his future. The whole Staten Island ferry service to Manhattan was changed when an enterprising group of men bought a steamboat, the *Nautilus*, and put it on the ferry trade.

Steamboats were not new. In 1807 Robert Fulton had successfully tested his first steamboat, the *Clermont*, on New York City's East River and then on the Hudson. That same year J. R. and R. J. Livingston, members of a prominent New Jersey family, built a steamboat called the *Raritan* to run between New Brunswick and New York. Fulton and the Livingstons went into partnership and secured a charter from the New York State Legislature to license steamboats all around New York. Soon they had licensed boats running in New York Harbor, on Long Island Sound, on the Great Lakes, and even in Canada.

While the state of New York was willing to license boats, the people of New Jersey did not approve of the idea. They did not like to have to pay New Yorkers for the privilege of running boats from their home towns to New York City, either. So they evaded the law.

One of the men who set up a rival shipping service from New Brunswick to New York was Thomas Gibbons, a rich Georgia planter who had come to the North several years before to live on an estate at Bottle Hill in what is now Madison, New Jersey.

By the end of the War of 1812 Thomas Gibbons was an important man in New Jersey. He owned part of the bank of New Brunswick, a number of businesses, and a great amount of land. When he first decided to go into the shipping business, he used a strange method. The *Raritan,* the steamer which belonged to the Fulton-Livingston monopoly, ran directly from New Brunswick to New York. But if Gibbons sent a boat directly to New York, the state authorities threatened to confiscate it and turn it over to the Fulton-Livingston monopoly for damages. So Gibbons ran a steamer to Elizabeth, New Jersey, just opposite Manhattan Island and then ran sailing boats across the bay. It was a troublesome way of doing business—all right for slow freight, but not satisfactory for passengers.

The New Brunswick-New York line was very important because it provided the shortest link between New

York City and Philadelphia, which also meant the shortest overland route to the south. Before the coming of steamboats the trip to Philadelphia had been made entirely overland—or on the long water route which meant much backtracking. Overland, the travelers had to go through the Jersey Meadows, stinking mudflats that were often almost impassable in the winter, and where hordes of mosquitos lived in the summer. The trip was long and uncomfortable, and might even be dangerous. So by 1817 nearly everyone who had to travel to Philadelphia chose the water route. Traveling on the *Raritan* or by Gibbons' ships to New Brunswick, they then disembarked, clambered into stage coaches for the fairly short ride across the New Jersey plain to Trenton, and then embarked in steamboats which carried them down the Delaware to Philadelphia.

For two years Corneel had been thinking about steamboats. Fulton and Livingston had four steamboats running the Hudson regularly. At first, having examined the boiler room and the capacity of a steamboat, Corneel had made a wrong guess. He decided that the machinery was too expensive and took up too much room which could be used, in a sailboat, for cargo or passengers.

In 1817, Corneel realized that he had been wrong and that the future of shipping lay in steamers. He took a day off from his work and rode one of the monopoly boats up to Albany and back, studying the machinery and the way the captain ran his vessel. He decided to go into steam.

At this time Thomas Gibbons was looking for a captain brave enough to help him fight the Fulton-Livingston monopoly by running directly to New York City from New Brunswick. The captain had to be a brave man, for he ran constant danger of arrest and imprisonment by the New York authorities who tried to enforce the monopoly. He must also be shrewd and active, to keep himself and his steamboat out of the hands of the police.

Thomas Gibbons heard of Corneel's exploits on New York harbor and asked him if he would be interested in the job. Corneel was interested. It offered him a chance to learn the ways of steam and to be paid for it. He would not have to risk any of his capital on the new steamboats until he was sure he could master the new trade. He could leave *Dread* and *Charlotte* and his other boats in the hands of his partners and still collect part of the profits. (At this time, Corneel had saved nine thousand dollars, a spectacular figure for such a young man.) He would not have to risk a penny of his cash and Gibbons would pay him sixty dollars a month while he learned steamboating.

Even more, Gibbons owned a hotel which stood next to the Raritan Hotel at the foot of Burnet Street, not more than a few yards from the spot where Corneel had sold his first load of shad in triumph. The hotel was old and run-down, a three story frame building. The Raritan house next door was a rough hostelry which catered mostly to sailors and stage coachmen. It was not a location for ladies and gentlemen, but it did have the advantage of lying near the steamboat terminal. Gibbons offered to lease the hotel to Vanderbilt if he and Sophia would run it as an inn for passengers from the Gibbons lines. Corneel agreed, without consulting Sophia, for he never consulted her on business matters even when her own affairs were at issue.

So they moved into the hotel, which Corneel christened Bellona Hall, after his new boat, a sidewheel steamer called the *Bellona*. Corneel, the new steamboat captain, was just twenty-four years old. It was the summer of 1818.

A few days after the move, Corneel set out at six o'clock one morning for New York in the new steamboat. He had a cabin full of passengers and a deck filled with cargo, and was bound for the forbidden waters of the monopoly territory. Aaron Ogden, who ran the rival line for the monopoly, sent a frantic warning to New York, telling the police that Vanderbilt was coming. But he did not know when or where Vanderbilt would dock, and that day Corneel escaped the eyes of the watchful dock officers, quickly unloaded passengers and cargo, took on those who wanted to return, and sped back to New Brunswick in time for supper.

That was the beginning of a cat-and-mouse game that was to last for several years. Corneel built a secret compartment in the hold of the *Bellona* and hid there when the New York police searched the ship, which was frequently. They were not interested in just taking the steamer. They had to prove that it had been sailed into New York waters illegally, and to do that they had to find the man who sailed it.

One time, when Corneel knew that the police would be waiting for him at the side of the pier, he brought a young women with him on the *Bellona* and coached her in docking the boat. What he really did was coach her in going through the motions of docking the boat, for his engineer was so well trained that Vanderbilt steered his boat into landing by thumping on the deck, just above the engineer's compartment. One thump with Vanderbilt's cane meant slow. Two taps meant fast. Three taps meant stop. That way, and with the girl pretending to steer the boat and give the orders, Vanderbilt brought the steamer into New York port on the day in question. As they approached the dock, Vanderbilt went into his secret compartment to hide, and when the police rushed aboard the ship, what did they find? Nothing but an engineer who appeared to be very stupid, and a young girl who said she had brought the ship into port. They couldn't very well arrest a girl, could they, without seeming very foolish? They never did find Vanderbilt on that trip.

One day they did catch Vanderbilt, however, and were surprised that a man of such fearsome reputation would be so quiet and subdued. Triumphantly they collared him and kept close watch on him until the time for the next steamer to Albany. They took him there, brought him before a judge, and prepared to confiscate the *Bellona* as booty.

The officers and the monopoly were surprised, however, when Vanderbilt pulled forth a paper which proved that on the day in question, when he had picked up passengers in New York bound for New Jersey, in violation of the law, the *Bellona* had been leased to Captain Tompkins, an officer who held a license to operate steamers in the New York waters. The judge was annoyed, and Vanderbilt was released by red-faced officers.

The years in New Brunswick were busy and prosperous ones for Corneel Vanderbilt and his family. The family was growing, too. Altogether, Corneel was to have a dozen children, most of them born during these years in New Jersey. He had so many children, in fact, that soon the family moved out of Bellona Hall, because they were taking up too many rooms which could be rented to paying guests. Vanderbilt then bought a house in the middle of the town, a brick-fronted house. He expanded the activity at Bellona Hall, too, turning it into a public house, or tavern, as well as a hotel for Gibbons' customers.

Corneel kept several teams of horses and a number of

carriages. In 1824, in fact, when the Marquis de Lafayette made a triumphal tour of America, and the city fathers of New Brunswick entertained him, the Marquis's splendid coach was drawn into the city by four pure white horses which belonged to Captain Vanderbilt.

For nearly twelve years Corneel stayed on in New Brunswick. Sophia looked after the hotel at the foot of the wharf, changing it from a rude stopping place to one of the best, if still plain, hotels in the region. There was plenty of business, for New Brunswick was the normal place for the stopover between New York and Philadelphia. Thomas Gibbons not only owned a steamboat line, but he owned stage coaches that took passengers to and from Trenton as well. The stage stop was nearly outside the door of Bellona Hall, and at boat time perhaps two or three dozen stages would line up along Burnet Street, waiting for the steamers to come in to discharge their passengers. Some passengers would leave late in the afternoon for the bumpy ride to Trenton, but many, particularly if there were ladies in the party, would choose to stay overnight at New Brunswick and rest before beginning the trip again the next day.

Captain Vanderbilt did not see much of the passengers who stopped over at his hotel. From early morning to late afternoon he was busy on the *Bellona* and the run to New York. He was a good steamboat captain. He knew the location of the shoals and the sand bars that threatened navigation. Like all the others, he loved to race, without giving much attention to the wishes or safety of his passengers.

Racing was a serious matter, too. The monopoly line discovered that Vanderbilt's *Bellona* was too fast for the old *Raritan* so they put new boats on the run, and eventually built the splendid *Legislature,* the finest boat on the Raritan River. Vanderbilt steamed in the *Bellona* for several years, but when the line prospered, Gibbons built the *Thistle,* a boat almost as luxurious as the *Legislature.* Then races were held in earnest. The idea was to persuade the passengers that the boat on which they were riding was the fastest of all. Then they would go home and tell all their friends about their speedy trip.

A race would begin at the wharf. Vanderbilt would arrive early and tell his engineer to get the boilers heated as fast as possible. Seeing the black smoke belching from the tall smokestack, the rival captain would know what Vanderbilt planned, and he would order full steam too. Then, when six o'clock came, and the passengers and freight were loaded, the lines were cast off. The first part of the race was for the vantage point of mid-channel in the Raritan. The winning boat would not have to dodge obstacles along the shallower bank. Once across the bar, in open water and heading for New York, the boats continued to gain speed. Vanderbilt learned to tie down the whistle of his steamboat, so not one drop of steam could escape, for the whistle also served as a safety valve to keep the pressure from growing too great.

Sometimes Corneel had accidents. One time in a race the boiler in his steamboat burst, but he was lucky—the boiler did not explode as they sometimes did, sinking the boat and blowing the passengers sky-high.

Usually, Vanderbilt won his races. He was a determined man. And usually, too, his passengers left the boat with great respect for him. He was every inch a captain, and his crew executed every order without slovenliness or argument.

It did not taken Corneel long to earn a good reputation. The monopoly line offered him a job at higher pay than he was getting from Gibbons. They offered him

$5,000 a year to sail for them. Gibbons was worried, because he did not want to lose his best captain. He said he would match the monopoly line figure. But Corneel refused the pay increase and refused to leave Gibbons either. He did not really need the money, for he was earning more from the restaurant and bar concession on his boat and from Bellona Hall than from his captaincy. He was gaining experience and that is what he wanted.

By 1825 the Gibbons line had grown and prospered. Many steamboat companies had sprung up around the New York area, particularly after Gibbons and Captain Vanderbilt made life so miserable for the monopoly that Ogden took the case to the United States Supreme Court, trying to stop the steamboats from competing with him.

This was a much more important case than it might have appeared on the surface. Involved here was the right of states to license and regulate interstate commerce. Vanderbilt and the other captains sailed between New Jersey and New York. Other steamboats, licensed by the state of New York, sailed into Ohio and into other states. New York even had the brashness to license a boat that sailed along the St. Lawrence River, between the United States and Canada! So it was not just interstate, but even international travel that might be affected by this law that was passed to be sure that Robert Fulton had the rewards he deserved for his invention.

The steamboat case was regarded by the Supreme Court as very important, too. Chief Justice John Marshall listened to the arguments, presented for the monopoly by a handful of important lawyers. For the Gibbons case, the company hired Daniel Webster, one of the most famous pleaders of all time. He and William Gibbons, the portly son of old Thomas, presented the Gibbons case.

In the end, Justice Marshall and the court decided that no state could regulate the right of steamboats to travel from one state to another. The exclusive franchises established by the Fulton-Livingston monopoly were outlawed. Captain Vanderbilt, by annoying the monopoly so much with his mischievous competitive tactics, had helped bring about an important court decision which would greatly affect the future of the whole country. For had the court decided the other way, the principle of competition would have been given a serious blow, and the whole development of America would have been slowed. Further, had the federal court not decided that the national interest was more important than any state interest, the Union might long ago have been dissolved. This was an issue of which Vanderbilt was not aware, because he was not a student of law or politics, but it was the issue to which Daniel Webster devoted the later years of his life—the strengthening of the Union at a time when it threatened to collapse from the narrow views the states took of their own interests.

In 1826 Thomas Gibbons died, a very rich man. He had been earning $40,000 a year or more from his steamboat line. He earned almost as much from his stage coach line. And after the monopoly was broken and it became possible to expand the steamboat line without danger, Gibbons' profits grew higher. So did Corneel's pay. But more important to Corneel was the freedom he gained as Gibbons' first captain. Corneel sailed only in the newest vessels, and soon he was not even bound by a regular schedule. He ran excursion trips which were so popular in those days and so profitable to the steamboat lines. Sometimes he would run up the Hudson River for a day, taking sightseers from New York. Sometimes the run would be to Atlantic City or on an evening tour of New

York harbor. Gibbons built new boats before he died, among them the *Bolivar*, which became Vanderbilt's charge.

But after Thomas Gibons died, the affairs of the Gibbons line did not prosper. William Gibbons was a lawyer, not a steamboat man. He had no interest in the sea, nor did he care how the line ran as long as it was profitable. After 1826, Corneel was really in charge of the Gibbons steamboat line, although he did not own any of it. He had several offers of better jobs, but he did not want to work for anyone else—and he was not quite ready to leave Gibbons.

Instead, Corneel made a compromise which let him prepare himself and await the best time for his own move, and still make profits. He sold some of his Staten Island sailboats and bought a steamboat called the *Caroline*. He was careful not to run the *Caroline* on the New Brunswick route, because he had no wish to antagonize Gibbons. Instead, the *Caroline* ran wherever there was money to be made, up and down the harbor carrying freight and passengers on excursions.

Corneel stayed on with the Gibbons line and learned more about the business of running steamboats. There was much to be learned, too. In the beginning, in 1817, Corneel had joined Gibbons with gusto in rate cutting and rampaging up and down the harbor. But Gibbons knew then, and Corneel did not, that where rates were cut below costs, the difference had to be made up somewhere. One way Gibbons made up the difference was to cut down on the accommodations for passengers, even on those things necessary for safety. Another was to raise the prices after the rate war was over. Another was to make up the prices in a different way. One time, during the war with Ogden, the rate for a trip from New Brunswick to New York fell from four dollars to twelve and a half cents. Obviously the money to support the steamboats had to come from somewhere. So the prices of food and drinks aboard the *Bellona* were raised enough so that Gibbons still made a profit from each trip.

Three years after the death of Thomas Gibbons, Vanderbilt decided to leave New Brunswick and the Gibbons line. William Gibbons had not paid any attention to the steamboat company. He had even told Vanderbilt that he might sell it if he got a good offer. What he considered a good offer, however, was far too much for Corneel, who saw no value in buying a going concern at high prices if he could build a business of his own.

There was a great deal of opportunity in steamboating at this time. New York was growing even more rapidly than it had before the War of 1812. To be sure, there had been a serious depression which lasted about five years at the end of the war, but in the 1820's the city began to prosper. The Erie Canal had been completed in 1825, opening the whole west to New York, since the canal connected Lake Erie to the Hudson River. That meant New York would be the center to supply the growth of the west. Factories up and down the Hudson and along Long Island Sound began to hum and as they turned out products, steamboats increased in number, for railroads were still in their infancy.

Looking around for an investment, Vanderbilt considered railroads. He traveled one night with a New Brunswick friend all the way to Jersey City to attend a meeting at which the future of railroading was discussed.

But in the end Corneel decided to stick with a business he knew, steamboating. Gibbons sold the old company out to the rival Ogden line, and Vanderbilt then had no hesitation about putting his *Caroline* on the

New Brunswick route in competition. The price war began, and lasted for several months. The fare was cut in half and cut in half again. Finally, the Ogden line managers, in desperation, offered to buy Vanderbilt off. They would pay him, they said, if he would leave New Brunswick and take his boats off the New Brunswick-New York run. Vanderbilt was never opposed to being paid for doing nothing, so he agreed. He packed up the children, nearly a dozen of them, and told Sophia they were going to live in New York. Then they loaded their furniture and their belongings on one of his steamboats, and set out for Manhattan Island. Corneel had served his apprenticeship. He was thirty-five years old and he was now Captain Vanderbilt, a tall handsome man who wore long sideburns and could drive a racing team as fast as anyone he knew.

That was to say nothing about what he could do with a steamboat, both in figuring how to make best use of it, and in driving it for every degree of speed possible when it was on the water. He was ready to attack the business world and earn a fortune.

~ 4 ~

THE COMMODORE

IT WAS 1829 when Corneel Vanderbilt and his family moved from New Brunswick to New York. Andrew Jackson had been elected President of the United States the year before.

The economy of the young nation had changed greatly in the past few months. Before 1828 America was a tiny farming nation. Business was dominated by merchants, who traded overseas for the manufactured goods that were not made in America.

But in 1828 the United States House and the Senate passed a bill which established a high tax on goods that were imported into the United States. The idea was to collect taxes for running the government and at the same time to protect the little industries of America, which were not so well-equipped or so experienced as to compete well with the older industries of Europe.

It was an exciting time to be moving to New York. That year a famous balloonist had made an ascension from Castle Garden, the best-known amusement spot in the city. The city was bustling. The new tariff laws had encouraged industry, so manufacturers of wool and cotton cloth were flocking to find factory space near the ports, yet to remain in the less expensive districts. Real estate had jumped in value. A lot on the west side of Broadway, the main street of New York, sold for $10,500. Of course that lot overlooked the old Bowling Green, which was used originally for bowling on the lawn, but now had become more a public park. Prices were rising in the city. Wood sold for $4.00 a load, which meant about a cord by today's standards. Martin Van Buren had been elected governor of New York in 1828, but he startled the people by resigning in March, 1829, to accept appointment as Secretary of State in President Jackson's cabinet.

And that year, old John Jay died at the age of eighty-four, recalling to many people of the city the great change that had come about in America in less than half a century. For a time, when New York had been the capital of the Confederation, Jay had been the most important man in the government. He was Secretary of State, and as such he was the one official who was not disturbed by constant political bickering and argument. Unlike many nations, which worried intensely about national problems and cared little for what others thought, the young United States had a sharp interest in the affairs of Europe even though it wanted no entanglement there. Jay had once served in France and in Spain as ambassador. When he returned to the United States at the end of the Revolution, his house in lower New York became the scene of many gay parties and much intrigue.

How times had changed! The old Dutch houses were being pulled down, and new brick and brownstone houses were going up—four stories and more, because the city was becoming so crowded that every foot of land was valuable.

Corneel Vanderbilt saw nothing of this. He moved his family into a shabby house on Stone Street. All that concerned him was that it be large enough to hold his huge family, and that it have stables in back for his carriages and fine horses. Other than that, New York was interesting to Corneel only because it gave him access to the water, and because it was a central point for the new steamboat traffic.

The steamboat had already changed shipping completely. Where before Corneel and others had loaded goods from the wharves and the tall-masted sailing ships into little sloops, the steamboats had now driven most of the sloops off the river and the coastal waters. Steamboats had so shortened the time it took to go from New York to points up the Hudson River that they had created new markets and new resorts, such as Saratoga Springs, which became so popular a few years later. The steamboat *Chancellor Livingston* puffed its way to Providence, Rhode Island, in seventeen and a half hours!

That first year Vanderbilt put his little steamboat, the *Caroline,* on the run up the Hudson River to Peekskill. He selected this particular route because it was short enough for a round trip to be completed within the daylight hours of a single day. Corneel did not have the boats or the capital to become involved in such expensive ventures as the New York-Albany run, for that would have meant he must have at least two large steamboats, and crews, and offices at both ends of the line.

Corneel did well in that first year. Robert Livingston Stevens, who had inherited great wealth and a part of the steamboat trade, had been working that line too, but Vanderbilt's competition was too much for Stevens. Vanderbilt did not hesitate to cut rates and to do everything else he could to make life unbearable for his competitor. Stevens withdrew from the route to more comfortable waters, an act that was not a disgrace, for routes were easy to find then. Corneel did not worry about the ethics of driving a competitor out of business. He was not much of a worrier, either then or at any other time. He had grown up in a school of thought that believed might makes right. He had served under a steamboat owner who was breaking the law of New York every single day, and so had learned to believe that law was not all-powerful. Once, when challenged by another person because he might be breaking the law, Corneel exploded. "What do I care for the law!" he said. "I've got the power."

Corneel was a harsh young man, and by our standards not a very honest or honorable man, but he must be judged within the framework of his own times. It was true that the real ladies and gentlemen of the day had much higher standards. Their word was their bond. They would not cheat or lie, nor would they stoop to take advantage of an associate. But these people were not in business. Their money came from land and from farming. Business, in those days, was a cut-throat proposition. Every businessman tried to take advantage of every other, and it was only by shrewdness and an ability for self-protection that any businessmen survived.

Take the case of Henry Astor: Henry Astor was a butcher. He had come to America with the Hessians during the Revolutionary War and had remained to become an American. He opened a slaughterhouse and began to supply New York with meat, while his brother John Jacob Astor went first into the fur trade and then into the real estate business in New York. Henry Astor, like John Jacob, never scorned a chance to cheat another man in a business deal—because it was not considered "cheating" in those days, but "shrewd dealing." One time, a young man named Daniel Drew came to Henry

Astor to sell some cattle. He had driven them down from the country, he said.

Were they nice and fat? Henry asked.

Fat as could be, smiled the lanky young man.

Henry Astor walked out and looked at the herd. They were fat ones, all right. There the cattle stood, chewing their cud, tails swishing, bellies bulged out.

All right, he said. He would take them at the top price of three cents a pound.

Daniel Drew walked away that day with a handful of money. When Henry Astor took the first cow into the slaughterhouse and cut its throat, he knew what had happened. He had been swindled. Drew had bought a scrawny, grass-fed herd somewhere in upstate New York and had driven them down to the Bowery. Somewhere along the line he had fed the herd great quantities of salt to make the cattle thirsty. Just before arrival at Astor's Bull's Head Tavern, he had stopped to water the beasts. Thirsty from the salt, the cattle had drunk until their sides bulged out, and Henry Astor had bought thousands of pounds of water, at three cents a pound.

Was Henry Astor so annoyed that he wanted to shoot Daniel Drew? Not at all. He was angry at first, of course, as was everyone who was swindled. But he realized that he had been outfoxed by Daniel Drew, and thereafter he went into business with the younger man and lent him the money on which Drew began to earn his own fortune.

That was how business worked. It was every man for himself and every man knew it worked exactly that way. So when Corneel went onto the Hudson River, what did he do? For one thing, he slandered his competitors unmercifully. He bragged in printed broadsides about the roominess and comfort of his boat and indicated that it was the most luxurious and fastest ship afloat. Of course, it was not. It was a tiny steamboat that could not even accommodate ladies properly.

The next year, 1830, Corneel had prospered so well that he was able to buy the old steamboat he had started with a dozen years before—the *Bellona*. He also bought a steamboat called the *General Jackson*. She was by far the largest boat Corneel had ever owned until this time. She measured one hundrd fourteen feet long, and she was twenty-two feet wide.

With the fleet of three steamboats, Vanderbilt was now an important businessman. He stayed behind in New York City now, thinking of ways to improve the business. Young Jake, his brother, was put in charge of the *General Jackson,* the pride of the Vanderbilt fleet, and the boat was placed on the Hudson River route.

Jake Vanderbilt was a daring young captain, just as his brother had been in his earlier days. He was twenty-three years old when he became captain of the *General Jackson,* but he had had experience in New Brunswick, working as a deck hand, and later as pilot for his brother, and finally as captain of one of the smaller Gibbons boats in the last year or two before Vanderbilt left the Gibbons line.

As a young captain who had been given great freedom by his older brother, Jake liked to race up and down the river as fast as the *General Jackson* would carry him. Sometimes he would bump into the wharf, frightening his passengers, or bump into the side of another steamboat, frightening both passengers and the other crew.

One day when Jake had been racing up the Hudson in his usual manner, the engineer warned him that the boiler was overheating, so he maneuvered to the shore at a point across from Grassy Point near Haverstraw and signalled for the engineer to stop the steam engine until the boiler could blow off some steam.

Just as the engineer was beginning to blow steam and relieve the pressure, the overburdened boiler gave way and exploded. Iron, wood, cloth, and bodies flew high in the air. The explosion was so strong it blew the bottom right out of the *General Jackson,* and it killed the engineer and eleven passengers who had been on deck above the weakened boiler.

The explosion aboard the *General Jackson* created a great outcry in New York. There had been a number of steamboat tragedies and the newspapers said most of them were caused by inferior materials used in the steamboats, carelessness of steamboat crews, and lack of skill.

Luckily for Vanderbilt, the *General Jackson* could be repaired but, unluckily, he could not put the big steamboat back on the Hudson River very quickly because too many people remembered her weak boiler and the tragedy. When the boat was repaired he decided to send it south, where he hoped nobody would remember the unfortunate accident at Grassy Point.

Captain Jake took the *General Jackson* to Norfolk, Virginia, planning to run from Norfolk to Richmond on round trips three times a week. However, the reputation of the *General Jackson* had come to Norfolk before her. Jake advertised that the boat was completely refinished and had a brand new boiler, a brand new bottom made of copper, and a low pressure engine, but still the people of Virginia refused to ride on his steamboat.

Jake sat at the wharf in Norfolk as long as he could stand it and made a few trips up the river, but the Virginians would not accept him. Then he tried to persuade them by offering cheap excursion trips from Norfolk to

Old Point Comfort at twenty-five cents for the trip. People who lived along the shore and along the rivers enjoyed steamer excursions, and on fine days, particularly on Sundays, steamboats would be packed with families and couples traveling off to see the sights and spend a pleasant time.

But even the excursionists distrusted the *General Jackson*. They stayed home, too. Finally Jake and Corneel became disgusted, so Corneel ordered Jake home to New York to see what could be done to make use of their most valuable steamboat.

In the meantime, the paths of Corneel and Daniel Drew had crossed for the first time. After the accident at Grassy Point, Daniel Drew had seen a good chance to make money in the steamboat business. He did not know anything about steamboats except that he was a regular passenger between New York City and his home town of Carmel, New York, on Vanderbilt's boats. Drew did know a great deal about business. He had already begun to speculate successfully in Wall Street.

After Jake Vanderbilt's accident, Drew bought a steamboat of his own and hired a captain to put it on the Hudson River run in competition with the Vanderbilt line. Drew's *Water Witch* was bigger and better than the other two Vanderbilt boats. Furthermore, Drew adopted Corneel's own method of competition. When Jake was trying to drum up trade for the *General Jackson* in Norfolk at twenty-five cents a trip, that is just what Drew was charging for the whole trip from New York to Peekskill. Vanderbilt bought another steamboat, the *Cinderella*, and the competition became fierce. Drew sent men out in the countryside above New York to warn the people that Vanderbilt's competition was dangerous. What Vanderbilt wanted, Drew said, was to keep prices low until all the competitors were forced off the river. Then Vanderbilt would raise prices sky-high, and the farmers would suffer because they would have no other way to ship their produce to market.

It was true that a steamboat monopoly would give the farmers no other way to ship. Railroads were just beginning to come to America. That same year, the Paterson (N. J.) Railroad company was formed and offered stock to the public. That stock was snapped up by eager buyers who realized that railroads would be important in transportation, particularly to areas in the country where steamboats could not run. The Paterson stock was offered in March, 1831. A few months later the New York and Harlem Railroad was formed. All its stock was bought up on the first day it appeared on the market, but not by Corneel Vanderbilt. He was interested in steamboats, not in railroads. Just as once he had believed the periauger was superior to the steamboat, now he believed his fortune lay in steamboats, not in the new-fangled railroads.

Corneel finally became concerned enough about Daniel Drew's competition that he paid Drew to stop running the *Water Witch* on the Hudson. Drew was glad to be paid off, for he had lost $10,000 in that first year of competition (a fact Corneel did not know).

A few months later, Corneel announced plans to expand his own service up the Hudson River to include a number of new points. In Albany, the Hudson River Association took violent exception to Vanderbilt's plans. The association was made up of steamboat men who did not compete with one another, and Vanderbilt proposed to compete with any number of them. They put their heads together, and then offered Vanderbilt a large sum of money to leave the Hudson River steamboat traffic alone. Vanderbilt again was happy to be paid without working for the money. In addition, Vanderbilt had designs on other routes which seemed more profitable. He planned to travel up and down Long Island Sound, between the farm and industrial areas of Connecticut, Massachusetts, Long Island, and the big city of New York.

When Jake returned to New York City with the *General Jackson,* Corneel put it on a run along Long Island Sound, between New York and Norwich, Connecticut, with stops at Saybrook, New London, and Sag Harbor on Long Island.

Vanderbilt prospered on Long Island Sound and he built more steamboats to cover more cities. Even during the terrible cholera epidemic of 1832 in New York, Vanderbilt continued to run his steamboat service between the city and the country towns. He carried hundreds of passengers out of the city that summer. Everyone who had any money at all or any regard for life left New York for the country, for men, women, and children were dying by the score in the city that year. Altogether a hundred thousand people fled New York that summer, leaving their homes prey to looters. They did not care as long as they could get away from the dreadful sickness that brought death. Vanderbilt carried many of these people in his steamboats, and when the epidemic was ended, and the cool winds of September drove away the rats which bore the disease, Vanderbilt cheerfully brought thousands of survivors back to the city in his steamboats.

These new steamboats of Vanderbilt were great improvements over the old ones, like his *Bellona.* The old boats had held only a single cabin, and the passengers sat on hard wooden benches or on their luggage as often as not. Outside on the deck the crew tethered cows and sheep and stacked produce and other freight. Passengers and freight were all mixed together and the average stamboat captain treated them just alike. That was in the early 1820's when there were only 300 steamboats in American waters. Ten years later, the number of boats had increased greatly. The types of steamboats were different, too.

Corneel designed some of his own steamboats and added some refinements to them, particularly insofar as engines and cargo handling were concerned. The passenger compartments were becoming more standard. On the biggest boats, which made overnight journeys, there were at least two different cabins for sleeping—one for women and one for men. In the cabins, the beds were double or triple bunks, lined up row after row. All the passengers in each room used the same washing facilities.

As time went on, more cabins were added for privacy, and the steamboats also added big dining saloons and even libraries and lounges. In the dining saloons each steamboat tried to outdo the others in the quality and quantity of its food. On the tables they served free whiskey in decanters. The ladies could have wine if they preferred. The prices changed for the trips, depending on the amount of competition. The trip from New York to New London might cost five dollars one day—the next day it might be cut two dollars if a price war began.

In 1832 Vanderbilt had bought the *Chancellor Livingston*, which was built by Robert Fulton in 1816, and had put it on the run up Long Island Sound. While he concentrated his efforts on the Sound, he did not stay off the Hudson River for very long, nor did he stay off the New Brunswick run. He and Daniel Drew formed a partnership for a time and ran steamboats all around the New York area. He went into business with other men, too, but mostly he kept to himself, kept his own boats and the profits, and then sank them into bigger and better steamboats. It was not long before he became known as Commodore Vanderbilt, a title honoring him as a merchant shipping king, and one he was to keep for the rest of his life.

In 1833 the new Commodore became seriously interested in railroads as an investment. As the Harlem Railroad and the Hudson Railroad spread out north and east from New York City, he could see that they would offer serious competition to his steamboats. Also, he was aware of the development of the Camden and Amboy Railroad, a little road which meant much to the Commodore because of his background as a steamboat man on the New York-to-New Brunswick run. Before Vanderbilt's days, the trip to Philadelphia had been extremely long and hard. In Vanderbilt's days on the Raritan, it had still been an arduous journey. But now, in 1833, a passenger for Philadelphia could board a steamboat at the foot of Manhattan Island at six-thirty in the morning and be in Philadelphia by two o'clock that afternoon. The steamboat would take him to Perth Amboy, just behind Staten Island. There he would board the train which would carry him south and west to Camden, only a ferry's journey from Philadelphia.

In the fall of 1833 Vanderbilt decided to ride the Camden and Amboy to see what changes had been made in the old transportation system. He boarded the train and sat back in one of the coaches to test this competing method of travel. Suddenly, when the belching engine was carrying them along at the racing speed of twenty-five miles an hour, one of the carriages up ahead jumped the track, and in a moment the entire train was derailed, lying on its side and sliding down an eighty-foot embankment.

Vanderbilt must have been traveling under a lucky star that day. Most of the passengers in his car were killed and many of the rest were badly injured. Vanderbilt was injured, too, with broken ribs and a punctured lung, but at least he was alive.

Rescuers carried him out of the wreckage and to a nearby farmhouse. Later, when Sophia was informed, she sent for Dr. Jared Linsly and asked him to go to Hightstown, where the accident had occurred, and take care of Vanderbilt.

After the doctor arrived, he had Vanderbilt moved into a private cottage. There he stayed for four weeks, his upper torso swollen and injured. One night Dr. Linsly bled him three times, in the fashion of the day, to relieve the swelling and Vanderbilt's pains.

At the end of four weeks, Vanderbilt was brought by horse cart and steamboat to New York, and then he spent another few weeks in bed getting his strength back. Then he went back to running his steamboats, but railroading stayed in the back of his mind. The accident did not bother him at all. Why should it? Vanderbilt steamboats had been involved in accidents just as serious, if not more so.

Every year Vanderbilt was adding boats to his fleet. He added the *Union* to the run up the Hudson. The Hudson River Association, seeing that he would not stay off the river, declared war. The advantage for passengers was that this competition cut the running time from Albany to New York to twelve hours. Of course it was not always the most safe twelve hours the passengers had spent. The rival captains raced all the way. Timid old ladies were assured that the steamboats really did not have any boilers in them. These old ladies asked because they had heard such frightening tales about the explosion of steamer boilers.

But the Vanderbilt boats did have boilers, and what boilers! Vanderbilt's captains tied down the safety valves and fed wood into the furnaces as fast as they would take it. Furnaces that were supposed to use eighteen cords of wood on the river trip were force-fed with twenty-five cords, and the boiler pressure was doubled from the normal twenty-five pounds to fifty pounds of steam.

Vanderbilt's steamers sometimes seemed to be more racing boats than passenger and freight carriers. The captains landed "on the fly," which meant that passengers who wanted to debark at some point between the two big cities would get into a launch which would then be let out on a long line behind the steamboat. The steamboat would approach the wharf, and then turn in and slow down but would not stop. The small boat would coast in to the wharf. Then the passengers were expected to land "on the fly"—to jump ashore before the rope tightened and the small boat was jerked away from the bank.

Boys and girls might love to watch this sport, and strong men might excel at it, but not all the passengers on the steamers were strong men. Over the years a number of women and children and old people were drowned landing "on the fly," and eventually the New York State Legislature passed a law forbidding this practice of Vanderbilt's.

By this time, Vanderbilt was a very important man in the steamboat business. It was not a joke for him to battle the whole Hudson River Association, but he had a few hidden weapons. He and Daniel Drew owned the Elizabethtown ferry and maintained ten vessels on it. It helped pay the expenses of the costly struggle on the river. Eventually, in behalf of the Association, Robert L. Stevens negotiated with Vanderbilt. They settled for a payment of $100,000 if Vanderbilt would go off the Hudson for ten years. In addition, he was to receive five thousand dollars for every year that he actually stayed off. It was easy to see that the Association had little trust in Commodore Vanderbilt.

In 1835 Commodore Vanderbilt built his finest steamboat up to that time, the *Lexington*. He ordered some changes in design, too. The *Lexington* had an engine at the beam, so efficient that it consumed about half the amount of wood that a steamer of that size usually used. Jake Vanderbilt, now chief captain for the whole line, ran the *Lexington,* and he soon gained a fearsome reputation as a man who would stop at absolutely nothing to win a race. One rival ship, in fact, once advertised that it would leave five minutes after the *Lexington* in order to prevent the danger of ramming (by Vanderbilt) and the loss of life at the dock.

The Commodore was the same as Jake. Sometimes the Commodore took the wheel of the *Lexington* and ran her swiftly between the dangerous rocks of Hell Gate, which separates New York Harbor from the Sound. Vanderbilt also told his captains never to stop for bad weather if they could go on. "If you can see ahead, go ahead," he said.

As the years went by, Commodore Vanderbilt continued to enlarge his shipping empire. In 1838 he bought the Staten Island ferry service and began to put some of his older boats on the short ferry run. In 1839 he and Daniel Drew established the New Jersey Steam Navigation Company. Some people thought this was a trick on Vanderbilt's part to get back into the Hudson River steamboat trade. And that is what it was. Soon the new company's boats were running on the Hudson, much to the chagrin of the Hudson River Association. But they were not Vanderbilt steamboats—technically—so very little could be done.

State governments paid little attention to such matters, for these were the days in which businessmen, no matter what their motives, were developing transportation routes and working as pioneers to help bring new ideas and better living to the country. Nearly everywhere one turned there was a frontier, whether it was in bringing ice to the British West Indies, or in rolling horsecars up the streets of Manhattan. Given an idea, and helped by some money behind him, a youngster could carve out a fortune in no time at all.

Commodore Vanderbilt had proved that. In 1840 he was forty-six years old and many times a millionaire. That year he completed a mansion on Staten Island, and on the glass front door was painted a picture of one of his steamboats. He had earned more in his lifetime than all the other Vanderbilts had earned in nearly three hundred years. And this was only the beginning.

~ 5 ~

NICARAGUA

THE STEAMBOAT whose likeness Commodore Vanderbilt
had painted on the front door of his Staten Island home
was the *Cleopatra*, launched in 1836, but in 1840 still one
of the finest of the American steamboat fleet. She was 193
feet long, and she carried two big smokestacks that
belched black smoke and sparks high in the air as she
steamed majestically along the Sound.

The *Cleopatra* had been built for the New York-New
Haven run. For a time Vanderbilt had run the old
Bolivar on that line, but one day an angry passenger
wagered another that he could drive from New Haven
to New York in a wagon and beat the *Bolivar*. He did it,
too, for the old *Bolivar* huffed and puffed and stopped,
it seemed to the passengers, at every inlet on the Connecticut and Westchester County shores.

Vanderbilt decided that he needed a new boat on a
non-stop run, and he put the *Cleopatra* on the route. At
the beginning of her working years the fare for one-way
passage between the two cities was two dollars. It dropped
to one dollar, however, on the days that the rival *Bunker
Hill* ran, for she was operated by another line. But Vanderbilt was always willing to make a business deal. One
time, another boat called the *Emerald* tried to compete

on the same New York-New Haven run. Vanderbilt and his competitors who owned the *Bunker Hill* ganged up on the *Emerald*. They cut the rates and operated as a team until the *Emerald* left the route in disgust. Then Vanderbilt and his competitors went back to their private feud.

Vanderbilt was fortunate in one way. He entered the steamboat business at the best possible time, and through his own efforts he grew with the area in which he lived at the time it was growing most. That does not mean he was simply lucky, for there were hundreds of others in the steamboat business, and he outfoxed them all. Part of the reason for his success was determination. Part of it was foresight.

In 1840 New York City boasted a population of 300,-000 people—more than ten times its size in the year that Corneel Vanderbilt was born. But the nation had grown even more remarkably and now numbered seventeen million persons, with most of the population centers scattered along the eastern seaboard, and a very large number of them within the range that Vanderbilt considered his personal transportation territory.

That was the year Vanderbilt put the *Lexington* on the New York-Norwich run. He was getting ready for the day when the Long Island Railroad would complete its terminal at Greenport, at the end of the island. Vanderbilt had shown foresight. Because he was interested in transportation in the area, he had bought a large amount of stock in the Long Island Railroad and sat on that railroad's board of directors. Undoubtedly he had some say in the movement of the railroad to the farthest points east on the island.

The Greenport terminal was completed in 1844. Then trains could leave Brooklyn at eight o'clock in the morning and travel to Greenport, more than one hundred miles east, in only a few hours. Travelers then could transfer at Greenport to the *Cleopatra*, the *Worcester*, or the *New Haven*, which traveled between the Long Island port and Norwich, to make connections with the railroads to Worcester, or to Stonington to make connections for Boston. In October that year, Vanderbilt sold the *Cleopatra* to the Long Island Railroad at a fine profit over her original cost.

The combination of railroads and steamboats was making the distances between the big cities of America seem very small. It now took only fourteen hours to travel to Boston, by way of the Long Island Railroad, Vanderbilt's steamers, and the Boston and Stonington line. That railroad had been built for the specific purpose of enabling passengers to escape the long and dangerous journey around Point Judith, where the winds and seas could never be counted on for safety.

As time went on the competition became more and more fierce. The railroads built their own steamships to compete with the steamboat operators. Why, they asked, should they run passengers from Boston down to Stonington, and then let Vanderbilt get a huge profit for taking them across the sound? Vanderbilt's answer, a few years later, was to buy the Boston and Stonington Railroad himself.

Another kind of competition sprang up on the Sound, too. The passenger steamers charged seven or eight cents a foot for hauling freight from New England to New York Port. Benjamin Buffum, of Providence, decided this was too high, and that he could profit by establishing a commercial steamboat line which did not cater to the whims of passengers, but carried freight only. So Buffum began his Commercial Steamboat Company and invested heavily in propeller-driven ships, a new variety. But Vanderbilt was not idle. Buffum's first ship sailed out of New England without a stick of freight aboard, for Vanderbilt had so cut the freight rates that no one wanted to pay two cents a foot when they could get it cheaper from him.

The Vanderbilts made it their business to know what was happening all over the area. One day the New York and Erie Railroad company decided it needed a freighter for ferry purposes. But it was difficult to find freighters and it seemed as though the railroad might not get one for some time. Jake Vanderbilt heard about the railroad's problem and acted quickly. He bought the *New Haven,* which the Commodore had sold to the Long Island Railroad for a good profit, and paid the railroad's price. Then he turned around the next week and sold the old *New Haven* to the New York and Erie for a good profit. He had done nothing except know where to go and how to get the steamboat.

In the spring of 1846 Commodore Vanderbilt engaged in a famous race with another steamboat "Commodore" —George Law.

George Law had followed a different path to achieve his fortune, but in many ways he was like the Commodore. He had grown up a poor boy in the country and in the 1820's had worked on the Erie Canal as a laborer. Within a few years he had saved enough money to begin contracting for parts of big construction jobs. He undertook construction of a part of the Croton reservoir and aqueduct system, which brought New York City its first supply of clean, fresh running water. He also built the high bridge across the Harlem River, which brought the water into Manhattan Island.

Law earned a huge fortune, however, when he took

over parts of the New York street railways system, and when he joined Vanderbilt and other busy men in the steamboat business on Long Island Sound. In the middle of the 1840's, Law decided he would build the finest steamboat afloat. He gave the orders to a shipyard, and the work began on a monster steamer which was to have every refinement known to shipping men in those days. The *Oregon*, as she was called, was 330 feet long—longer than a football field. She was thirty-five feet wide at the beam, and she weighed a thousand tons. The distance from the cabin on the main deck forward to the bow was two hundred feet.

The *Oregon* boasted a barber shop on board and wash rooms for ladies and gentlemen, with huge washbowls cut from marble slabs. She could carry six hundred passengers in comfort, more than any other steamboat of her day. In the main sleeping cabin for men two hundred berths were placed end to end. Each berth was covered with fine sheeting, the finest woollen blankets, and French quilts into which had been worked the name of the steamboat.

The ladies' cabin was even finer than the men's, with satin curtains and a clock built into a stained glass wall at one end of the cabin. Next to the ladies' cabin were located the private staterooms which were elegantly furnished with overstuffed furniture and painted in white enamel and gilt with raised flowers of boiserie on the gilded pillars. The boat even boasted a bridal suite, which was the most expensively furnished of all.

Once the *Oregon* was completed, George Law put her on the New York-Albany run as the night boat in opposition to the Hudson River Association steamers. He started with a cut-rate fare of one dollar for the passage, but within a few weeks the fare had dropped twenty-five cents for the trip, so grim was the competition. Law bore that for several months, but when the winter came and with it the partial blocking of navigation by the ice that formed in the river, Law took that excuse to move the *Oregon* off the Hudson and into Long Island Sound where the salty water did not freeze and where the competition was not quite so stiff.

The Stonington run was an important one in those days. Stonington was tucked behind Fishers Island in the Sound, safe from the turbulence of the Atlantic most of the time. Until the New Haven Railroad was completed, Stonington was the major transfer point for travelers moving between Boston and New York. It was a brisk traffic and several steamboats, including Law's and Commodore Vanderbilt's, plied that route. Of course where there were rival steamboat captains there were steamboat races, because captains liked to race, and because winning races made good advertising for the steamer lines of the winning boats.

One day in June, 1846, Law's *Oregon* and Commodore Vanderbilt's *Traveller* raced for twenty miles along the route, covering the distance in fifty-seven minutes. They were so evenly matched that both claimed victory, and since it had been an impromptu race, no one could say for certain who was right.

In May, the next year, the *Bay State* defeated the *Oregon* in a longer race. George Law complained that it was a fluke, and that his steamboat could outrun anything afloat. He offered to bet $1,000 against anyone who would match the bet that the *Oregon* could win any kind of race.

Commodore Vanderbilt was always a gambling man. In fact his favorite pastime was whist, a popular card game of the nineteenth century, and his other avocation was trotting horses, on which he bet with great regularity. He could not let such a challenge go unanswered, particularly when there was so much glory at stake. So Vanderbilt answered Law's challenge and offered to race in his newest and finest steamboat, the *Cornelius Vanderbilt*.

The course was set along the Hudson River, from the tip of Manhattan to a point opposite Ossining, forty miles up the Hudson. The two boats were to start from the Battery and return there.

A huge crowd gathered at the foot of Manhattan on the morning of June 1, 1847, because Vanderbilt's boat was also going to be placed on the Stonington run, so many in New York wanted to know which of the two steamboats was the faster.

Just before eleven o'clock that morning, Vanderbilt's boat appeared off the Battery, with the Commodore standing on the bridge, stick in hand, smoking a cigar. George Law moved to the helm of his own boat, and at 10:56 a starting gun was fired and the two boats were off, churning up the Hudson side by side.

At thirty miles, three quarters of the way up the course, the *Cornelius Vanderbilt* gained a slight lead. She seemed to be the faster boat. Then, after Law demanded more steam, the *Oregon* spurted ahead. Vanderbilt steered the *Cornelius Vanderbilt* against his rival's boat and fouled her starboard side wheel as she passed. That was a trick, but not an unexpected one. Steamboat racing had no rules, except to win.

Fortunately for Law the fouling did not injure the paddle wheel of the *Oregon* or the race would have ended right there. Law kept his steam up, and in his erratic maneuver Vanderbilt lost some speed, so at the turn around the stake boat at Ossining, the *Oregon* was a little bit ahead. They were one hour and thirty-five minutes out of the Battery.

Seeing his opponent in the lead, Vanderbilt became excited and took the wheel away from his pilot. He began issuing orders to the engine room so quickly that the engineer was confused and feared that something had happened on deck. He stopped the engines, and at that moment, seeing what had happened, George Law ordered every bit of steam he could get to forge ahead.

Vanderbilt swore and stamped his cane on the deck and ordered full steam ahead. The *Oregon* stayed ahead all the way down the river to Yonkers, a few miles above Manhattan. There George Law discovered that his engineer was running out of wood, because he had demanded so much steam earlier. What should he do?

At this point, money was no object to George Law and winning the race was everything. He had spent $30,000 furnishing the *Oregon* with the finest in chairs, tables, stools, and woodwork afloat. Now he ordered everything that would burn to be fed into the furnaces of the *Oregon* to make steam. It was done. The magnificent berths were torn apart. The white enamel and gilt of the woodwork came down. The polished chairs were cut apart, and all were thrown into the furnace.

Now the *Oregon* pulled even farther ahead to win by a quarter of a mile as she steamed over the finish line across from the Battery.

It was a bitter defeat for Vanderbilt, but by the next year it was long forgotten because of an event that was to change the course of history in many ways. Gold was discovered in California, and the western coast of America, which had been half forgotten, suddenly became the promised land.

The problem of transportation was the most serious of all as far as development of this gold discovery was concerned. It took many months to cross the land by horse or by wagon train, and travel overland meant that the travelers ran constant danger from attack by hostile Indian tribes. The only other way to travel to California was by ship, and that meant boarding a ship on the east coast, sailing south, far south, around the southern tip of South America, and then back up the west coast to San Francisco Bay.

There was still another way to make the trip, now that there was sufficient interest in the route to attract enough traffic to make it pay for the shipping companies. The connecting link between North and South America thins out at Panama, and there it was less than fifty miles from Atlantic to Pacific oceans. It was possible to run one set of steamers from New York to Panama, and another set from Panama to San Francisco, thus eliminating more than half the long voyage around Cape Horn.

The first to see this possibility was a group of men which included George Law. They went to Congress, secured a mail subsidy, and formed the Atlantic and Pacific Steamship companies to carry mail and passengers by this route.

It took time, of course, to do this. In 1849, 750 ships sailed from the east coast for the west, carrying 100,000 passengers around the cape. Commodore Vanderbilt realized that he could not compete with Law and the others on their own grounds, since he did not have a mail subsidy as they did. So he drew up his own plan, which was even more daring than that of the other steamboat men. Vanderbilt decided that he would build a canal across the isthmus, not at Panama, but further north, where Lake Nicaragua pushes almost to the sea. The canal would connect the Pacific side with the lake. From the Atlantic side, the steamboats would move up the crooked San Juan River. Vanderbilt's canal would not let his ocean-going steamers travel from one coast to the other, but it would speed transport a great deal, cutting five hundred miles and perhaps five days from the trip through Panama. He planned to keep one set of ships running along the east coast and another set along the west, as did his competitors. But he would carry passengers aboard river steamers up the San Juan, across Lake Nicaragua, and triumphantly down his canal into the Pacific.

Then Vanderbilt had an even better idea. If he could get some support from really wealthy bankers, he could build a canal that would carry ocean-going vessels across the isthmus. There would be no need to trans-ship freight and passengers at all. It would save time, trouble, and above all, money.

In 1849, with all the interest and activity in the canal idea, the British suddenly showed interest in negotiating for settlement of some outstanding problems in South American between Britain and America. The result was the Clayton-Bulwer Treaty of 1850, which made it impossible for Americans to build any canal without the agreement of the British.

In 1850 Commodore Vanderbuilt took his first trip to Europe to consult with British bankers about lending money for the canal. The British could see no particular value to the canal, nor did they believe that shipping between the west and eastern coast of South and North America would be of enough importance to justify the tremendous expense involved. (After all, it was nine years before Ferdinand de Lesseps would begin construction of the Suez Canal, and all such projects seemed far too vast for bankers to contemplate.)

Bering Brothers, the banking firm, refused to have anything to do with the project, so Vanderbilt came home to try another approach.

He signed a contract with the Nicaraguan government for an exclusive franchise to run transportation across the isthmus and on Lake Nicaragua. He would try to build a canal, he said, but that might be impossible, and if that proved to be the case, he would use a combination of river steamers and mule-drawn carriages to carry passengers and freight across the isthmus.

He built a fleet of big blue carriages and a road on which they might travel across the twelve mile land gap between Lake Nicaragua and the Pacific Ocean. He made preparations to send a lake steamer, *Central America,* onto Lake Nicaragua accompanied by the smaller river boat *Director.*

The natives said that the San Juan River was too shallow for anything but canoes, and that the Castillo Rapids would tear the bottom from Vanderbilt's boat. They shook their heads and crossed themselves and were sure that Vanderbilt would drown himself.

Vanderbilt was not dismayed. On New Year's Day, 1851, he celebrated the holiday by going aboard the *Director,* taking the wheel, and navigating his boat up the river 119 miles to the open water of Lake Nicaragua.

Having proved that it could be done, Vanderbilt went home again to tend to his shipping empire and let other men do the day-to-day work of carrying passengers and freight across the isthmus.

Scarcely ten years before, a New York newspaper had speculated that Commodore Vanderbilt might be worth $250,000. How little the newspapermen knew. At this time, ten years later, Vanderbilt must have been worth five million dollars, for he earned a hundred thousand dollars a month from his steamboats alone.

Vanderbilt then sent out a fleet of steamships, bigger than the ones he used on Long Island Sound and the Hudson River for the most part, although some of the older boats were put on the California run. For a time, he called it the People's Opposition Line because it was in competition with George Law's Pacific Mail Steamship Company. He hired brave and reckless men to man his ships. They had to be both brave and reckless, for it was a dangerous trade. This can be shown by the story of the *Yankee Blade,* one of Vanderbilt's California steamers.

Strictly speaking the *Yankee Blade* was not totally a steamship. She carried three masts and nine sails and two jibs, besides the steam engine and side wheels which were her main source of power. The early steamers were thus equipped for ocean travel so that in case they found a following wind they could take advantage of it, and if their steam power broke down they would not be totally helpless.

The *Yankee Blade* was built by Perrine, Patterson, and Stack, a New York shipbuilding concern. Her stack was tall. It reached halfway up the main mast. She carried three boats on each side as a safety factor, and she was 274 feet long over all.

Vanderbilt bought the ship from the New York and San Francisco Steamship Company, or rather, he acquired it by swallowing that company after the *Yankee Blade* had made her first voyage south. Vanderbilt combined his company with the other, changed the name to the Nicaragua Steamship Company, and went to work to increase his fortune, doubling his number of ships in the California trade.

On February 2, 1854, the *Yankee Blade* sailed from New York to San Francisco, around Cape Horn, to join the *Uncle Sam* on the run between San Francisco and San Juan del Sur on the Pacific Ocean. Other Vanderbilt ships sailed between New York and San Juan del Norte on the Atlantic side.

On one of her earliest voyages the *Yankee Blade* ran out of coal and anchored near Coiba Island, off the coast of Central America. A rival vessel, the *Sonora,* passed her en route to Panama. The *Yankee Blade* made distress signals, but the *Sonora* went right by, violating one of the rules of the sea in her interest in competition. The captain of the rival *Sonora* was generous enough, however, to report the position of the *Yankee Blade* when he arrived in Panama. A steamer was just setting forth to look for the stricken ship when she came steaming into the harbor. Having been stranded without help, the crew and passengers helped themselves. They took boats ashore to Coiba Island, cut wood enough for the voyage, and hauled it back to their ship. Then they raised steam and headed for port.

All went well for a few months for Vanderbilt's *Yankee Blade,* but then in September, 1854, she set sail from Nicaragua as usual, only to have the crew discover when they were well at sea that they were carrying cholera aboard the ship! Before the ship arrived in San Francisco sixteen crewmen and passengers died.

That was not the end of her troubles. After the *Yankee Blade* had been scoured and cleared for sea once again, she set sail on September 30, carrying eight hundred passengers and several hundred thousands of dollars worth of gold and silver from the California mines. The next day, off the California coast she ran into dense fog, but instead of lying to and waiting for the fog to lift, the captain obeyed Vanderbilt's orders to forge ahead. Feeling her way, she struck a rock at Point Arguello, fifteen miles from Point Conception. The rock came as a huge surprise, for the captain thought they were at least ten miles offshore, and actually they were just a few yards from shore.

Just after the *Yankee Blade* struck, headwinds and

swells combined to drive her sixty feet onto the reef. In half an hour the stern had sunk and water covered her as far as the promenade deck.

Instead of staying with his ship, the captain went off in a small boat to find a safe place to land the passengers and crew. While he was gone, the passengers panicked. The other boats were lowered and supplies were broken out and piled on the forward deck. The purser tried to break into the strong box, where most of the gold and silver was kept, but that box was kept on a lower deck and was already covered by five feet of water when he began his efforts to save the money.

In a little while the water began rising at the rate of six inches a minute. The ship had struck at four o'clock in the afternoon. By dark the surf had washed away the deck houses and lay heavily on the promenade deck as far forward as the air shaft. Passengers began slipping off into the boats and heading for the shore.

Darkness prevented the ship's boats from taking off all passengers, although the captain returned from his explorations before dark and began the rescue of the stranded.

When morning came on October 2, the work was resumed until eight o'clock when the *Goliath* happened to pass by and came to the rescue, taking off all the remaining passengers and rescuing those who had been put ashore already. But since the *Goliath* was heading the wrong way—back to San Francisco—some of the passengers preferred to remain ashore and wait for another rescuer. (A few days later they found one. They were picked up by a sailing ship and taken to Panama.)

That was the end of the *Yankee Blade*. On the night of October 2, a handful of castaways, waiting for southbound rescue, watched as the steamer broke up on the rocks and sank down beneath the waves. She carried with her most of the belongings of the eight hundred passengers and $153,000 in gold and silver which had been stored in the strong box.

Strangely, although her wrecking and rescue were among the more confused annals of the sea, only thirty lives were lost, and these men were drowned when the first officer's boat capsized during the rescue operations, and the men were dragged out from shore by the strong Pacific undertow.

If that was the end of one of his ships, still the Commodore had plenty more to work with, and he worked them hard. If there was a basis for complaint about his transportation line to California, it was not that he did not provide enough ships, but that he jammed passengers aboard them like livestock and manned his ships with catch-as-catch-can crews. But in this Vanderbilt was not unique. These were the days of "shanghaiing" and the "Mickey Finn." Miners and travelers risked their lives when they lingered on the Barbary Coast of San Francisco, for they might find themselves on their feet one minute, and drugged and lying in the stinking crew's compartment of an outbound ship a few hours later, on their way to Australia or around the horn to New York, or even for the China coast. Vanderbilt was not unique in his disregard of life, safety, and comfort of his passengers. Those were hard times and it took hard men to survive in them.

～ 6 ～

PASSAGE TO EUROPE

In the spring of 1853 Commodore Vanderbilt found himself to be a very rich man. He told an acquaintance that he was worth $11,000,000 and that he had it so well invested he drew twenty-five percent income on the money. Much of the money, of course, was invested in businesses he owned or at least controlled, like the Accessory Transit Company, his ferries, and his steamboat lines on Long Island Sound. Vanderbilt, then, was well satisfied with what he had accomplished in the first fifty-nine years of his life.

Now, for the first time, he decided it was proper to take a long vacation. He planned a trip to Europe. First, he built a yacht which cost a half million dollars, but neither this cost nor the trip itself was to prove to be purely pleasure before he was finished. There was another part of Vanderbilt's pattern of success. He never did anything just for pleasure, unless it was to go driving in his carriages or on a summer's visit to Saratoga Springs to escape the heat of New York City.

He put the affairs of Accessory Transit in the hands of two trusted employees. One was to take care of business at the New York City end of the line, the other was ordered to take charge of Vanderbilt's affairs in San Francisco.

He sold the Staten Island ferry that year for $600,000 and invested the money again where he thought he could make even more.

He employed Dr. Linsly to come on the trip to Europe to take care of all the passengers. He asked a Baptist minister to come along also. Then he issued invitations to all the members of his family except Cornelius Jeremiah Vanderbilt, his second son, and a daughter who was ill.

When the *North Star* was finished it was one of the largest and finest steamers afloat. She was 270 feet long, and the cabins were equipped with all the latest and finest furnishings, including a marble-topped coal stove to keep the passengers warm in the cold evenings.

On May 19, 1853, all was ready. A professional crew had been assembled. Also aboard in the forecastle were a number of young men from good families, who had signed on for this one voyage to participate in the Commodore's exploits. For while the Commodore was going to Europe on pleasure, still he proposed to make this a "goodwill" voyage, too. The newspapers commented that this trip would let Europe see how wealthy Americans lived. Most of the newspapers were very pleased that Vanderbilt planned to travel to England, France, Italy, through the Mediterranean, and even to Russia, for the wealthy families in all those countries had tended to look on the Americans as colonials—even though the Revolution was half a century behind them.

Captain Asa Eldridge was the man Vanderbilt selected to take charge of his new ship. Captain Eldridge was an able and experienced sailor. He had served Vanderbilt in the California trade. He had also sailed to India and to China. With his black beard and stern gaze, he was just the man needed to impress the crew with his strength and the notables they would meet abroad with his dignity and bearing.

Several hundred friends and acquaintances of Vanderbilt and the family were invited to join the party on the morning of departure and ride to the end of New York Harbor at Sandy Hook, where they would be met by a smaller Vanderbilt steamer and brought back to the city.

At 10:30 that morning the *North Star's* propellers began to turn, but in taking the ship out of the harbor the harbor pilot made an error, and three minutes later the *North Star* had run aground. Within a few hours she had been hauled into drydock to be examined for damage. Luckily, there was no serious damage, so the ship was ready to sail again the next day, but the party had been ruined.

Now, on May 20, another problem arose. The firemen who stoked the coal into the blazing furnaces decided they would strike for higher wages. They were sure it was too late for Vanderbilt to find another "black gang." They knew he was impatient to leave.

But the firemen did not know their employer. Commodore Vanderbilt would not be pushed by his workmen—not one inch. Immediately, he ordered the offenders off his ship and sent Captain Eldridge word to hire another crew from the gangs that hung around the wharves. If he had to pay higher wages, he would not pay them to men who tried to blackmail him.

That day, May 20, the ship did sail. Although the party's spirits were dampened by the trials of the past two days, when the *North Star* moved out toward the Narrows and past the old Stapleton cottage where Phebe Hand still lived, Vanderbilt unleashed a display of fireworks and small arms fire to hail his mother and tell her they were on their way. Then the boat headed for the open sea.

At the end of the harbor the pilot was put ashore with a purse filled with gold pieces in his hand to show the people that Vanderbilt had no hard feelings. Then the voyage really began.

The voyage across the ocean took eleven days. On June 1, the *North Star* docked at Southampton, and the Vanderbilt party left for London, to see and be seen.

The trip to London, however, was a social failure. Vanderbilt had hoped to receive some recognition from royalty, or at least from some of the noble families of the kingdom, but they ignored him. The newspapers marveled at the yacht, and at Vanderbilt. The London *Daily News* said it thought it was time for millionaires to stop being ashamed of having made their own fortunes, even if they earned them in common trade. Vanderbilt agreed with this idea, but the wellborn English did not. So the Vanderbilts were forced to amuse themselves in London. They visited Ascot to see the English horses race. They drove through the parks and around Buckingham Palace. They went to the Opera. They went to Madame Tussaud's famous waxworks to see lifelike reproductions of famous men and women of history. But they were not entertained by British society leaders. George Peabody, an American banker (and partner of J. P. Morgan's father), asked them to his suburban house. The American minister gave a party for them. But they were snubbed for the most part.

Then Vanderbilt took the party to Russia, sailing the *North Star* through the North and Baltic seas to the northeast coast. In Russia the Vanderbilts were treated very well. They rode in the Czar's own carriage and the Grand Duke Constantine came aboard the *North Star* for a visit.

After leaving Russia, the party sailed for France. Next, having seen the sights in Paris, the party then moved on to Spain, then to Italy, where a visit to Rome was cancelled because the city was suffering a bout with the plague. To make up for the disappointment, Vanderbilt took the party to Constantinople, where the Turks entertained them far more royally than had any but the Russians. Then, more than four months after the trip had begun, the *North Star* headed for Gibraltar, and then for New York.

On the homeward voyage, off the coast of Spain, a tragedy marred what had otherwise been a pleasant and safe voyage. Robert Ogden Flint, son of a prominent physician in Boston, had hired on as one of the members of the crew as an adventure. But in rough weather he was swept overboard and drowned. That was the single tragic event in the voyage, or so it seemed at the time.

When the Commodore arrived back in New York, he discovered that the two men he had employed to watch his interests in Nicaragua and San Francisco had betrayed him. Vanderbilt had selected Charles Morgan, a steamship operator from South Carolina, to handle the New York end of his business. He had hired Cornelius Garrison to work for him in San Francisco. Now the pair had decided to try to take over the Nicaragua business for themselves and had gone about sabotaging Vanderbilt's interests.

Cornelius Garrison, in a way, was the shrewder of the two. He had been a banker in Panama, and he spoke Spanish and knew the people of the area. He was so valuable that Vanderbilt paid him a salary of $60,000 a year.

But Garrison and Morgan were not content with salaries. They saw how it might be possible to take over the whole Vanderbilt line in Nicaragua, and they set out to do so. By the time Vanderbilt returned in September,

1853, Morgan and Garrison had seized control of the Accessory Transit Company. They refused to pay Vanderbilt twenty per cent of every passage across Nicaragua. They began hauling passengers to and from Nicaragua's shores in ships of their own, ignoring Vanderbilt's Pacific and Atlantic steamers. Since the agents controlled the Accessory Transit offices on both the Pacific and Atlantic side of Nicaragua, there seemed to be little that Commodore Vanderbilt could do.

The Commodore filed suits in court, as Morgan and Garrison had expected. They settled down, then, for a long court battle, in which they fully expected to be able to hold out for years.

But Vanderbilt did something else, too. He converted the *North Star* to a passenger steamer. (Many of his acquaintances had fully expected him to do this.) He also took several other steamers and formed an Opposition Line to California. This line competed with the lines of Garrison and Morgan, and with the United States and Pacific Mail companies as well. Then Vanderbilt cut the price of steerage passage to $35 from San Francisco to New York, and his two former associates knew they were in for a fight.

These new Vanderbilt ships were big and fast. They made the voyage from San Francisco to New York in twenty-one days. And at Vanderbilt's cut-throat prices, the waiting lists for travel on his ships were endless, while the business of the other shipping lines fell off.

Garrison and Morgan gave in within a few months. In the fall of 1854 Vanderbilt felt that he had won his battle. He moved his own ships back onto the Nicaraguan line, using Accessory Transit Company for travel across the isthmus once again. Garrison and Morgan paid his claims in full, which gave him hundreds of thousands of dollars in profits. He sold the *North Star* to George Law's United States Mail Company, since Vanderbilt regarded her as too big and too expensive for the California trade.

Vanderbilt had built the *North Star* for $500,000. He had sailed her across the ocean, taking twenty-one members of his family on vacation. He had brought the ship back and used it as a passenger liner for a year, and largely because of its speed and luxury had brought his enemies to their knees. Then he sold the ship to George Law for $400,000. It is apparent that the $100,000 difference did not represent any loss at all to Commodore Vanderbilt.

Vanderbilt continued to fight to regain control of the whole of the Accessory Transit Company. The one way he could do it was to become again a director of the company and an operating executive. Vanderbilt moved to do just that, and in 1855 he again became a director of the company.

That year Morgan and Garrison saw that if they were to defeat Vanderbilt and win control of the Nicaragua line, they would have to take some other measures. Slowly but surely Vanderbilt was winning back control of Accessory Transit.

Within Nicaragua, political affairs apparently played into the hands of Morgan and Garrison. In those days of unrest in Latin America, there had grown up a breed of men in the United States who were known as *filibusters*. Sometimes for glory, sometimes for money, and sometimes spurred by a strange patriotism, these filibusters tried to create revolutions in "banana Republics." They overthrew the existing governments and established governments of their own, to last until they, too, were overthrown, perhaps by other filibusters, or through the intervention of the United States or Great Britain.

Those two nations were then struggling for economic protection and influence in Latin America.

In the spring of 1855, one of these filibusters named William Walker gathered a small band of soldiers of fortune around him and sailed to Nicaragua, to return the banished Federico Castellón to the Presidency. Castellón had been exiled from Nicaragua by the new President Fruto Chamorro, after an election that meant as little as most Latin American elections of those days. Once Walker arrived in Nicaragua, he began gathering around him the enemies of Fruto Chamorro. And to assure some monetary support for his revolutionary attempt, Walker promised Morgan and Garrison that if they would ship him arms and men from the United States, he would take the charter and physical property of Accessory Transit away from the Vanderbilt company, and allow Morgan and Garrison to form their own company. The new company would be given the exclusive right to transport men and freight across the Nicaraguan route.

Garrison and Morgan were pleased to cooperate with William Walker. In the fall of 1855 they gave Walker $20,000 and a steamboat with which to transport his army across Lake Nicaragua. Commodore Vanderbilt did not know, at the moment, that they had given Walker Accessory Transit money or the permission to use the Vanderbilt lake steamboat named *La Virgen,* which was used to carry passengers across Lake Nicaragua on their way to California. Before Vanderbilt could learn of the treachery of his two assistants, Walker had acted.

On the night of October 11, the steamer was lying at the dock in the town of LaVirgen. Captain Scott was aboard, but he did not know that the Accessory Transit agent, C. J. Macdonald, had given Walker and his men permission to use the steamer. All was quiet on Lake Nicaragua and the steamer was waiting for passengers when the time for action came.

Walker came aboard with his men and his own steamer captain. He ordered Scott to surrender the ship, and he then prepared to take it across the lake to seize Granada, the capital of the Castellón government.

The lake steamer left port at 10:00 P.M., and steamed across the silent lake. At three o'clock on the morning of October 12 the steamer dropped anchor just outside Granada, and the desperate men of William Walker went ashore in a launch.

Walker had only a handful of men with him, but he needed no more to take the city, for President Chamorro's government was caught unawares, and most of the military men of Granada—the police—were either off duty or asleep in the *calabozo*. So Federico Castellón became President of Nicaragua and William Walker became commander of his armies and man behind the throne.

Early the next year, Commodore Vanderbilt again became president of Accessory Transit, but by this time it was too late to put an end to the first round of the battle. Morgan and Garrison had won that round. Their prize was the transfer of the charter for travel across Nicaragua from Accessory Transit to a new company they formed.

Now Morgan and Garrison were able to transport men across the isthmus to their own profit—but Vanderbilt, who controlled the ships at the New York end personally, simply ordered all of his ships to stay at the dock. Garrison was able to send some ships from San Francisco, but the arms and supplies that Walker would need to support his forces were available on the east coast, not on the west coast. And when Garrison sent an Accessory Transit ship from San Francisco, the Commodore's agents met it at the Nicaragua end of the line and directed the captain to proceed on south to Panama.

Vanderbilt's plan was to blockade William Walker as completely as possible, but as the battle continued, Morgan began to send ships and Garrison began to get ships through from the eastern end. Accessory Transit Company stock, now that there was no passage across Nicaragua, began to drop alarmingly.

To keep the company in business, Vanderbilt bought ships that were ordered up for sale and started a counter revolution against William Walker. He sent a pair of agents to the area. He persuaded the nations of Honduras, Guatemala, San Salvador, and Costa Rica to ally themselves against Walker—who had now succeeded Castellón as President of Nicaragua.

Vanderbilt's men secured the assistance of soldiers from these nations and marched into Nicaragua. By New Year's day, 1857, his troops controlled San Juan del Norte and the main link of the Accessory Transit route across the isthmus. Walker was isolated, and in a few months he was forced to surrender to an American naval officer and leave Nicaragua.

Later that year Walker re-entered Nicaragua with another force, but was quickly cut off and bottled up. He again surrendered and left Nicaragua, this time for good.

Vanderbilt now played Accessory Transit, and his right to travel across Nicaragua, against his competitors on the Panama run. But he decided not to put Accessory Transit back into business again. Thus, since the company's affairs were entirely in his hands, he sold Accessory Transit ships to himself at prices he felt he could afford to pay. Since Accessory Transit was a Nicaragua corporation, the stockholders could not even sue him.

The Commodore never did go back on the Nicaragua

run. For a time, his competitors on the Panama run paid him $56,000 a month not to run any ships south. Then they tired of this extortion and stopped. Vanderbilt started a new company in 1859, bought out the United States Mail line, and sailed from New York to Panama, leaving the other half of the service to the Pacific Mail Steamship Company. But even this was to last only a short time, for the government stopped subsidizing mail runs through Panama when it became possible to use stagecoach and horsemen over the overland route.

But true to his own tradition, Commodore Vanderbilt had not allowed himself to be caught napping by this change in affairs. As early as 1853, although he had denied any interest in trans-Atlantic crossings, Vanderbilt had been planning a trans-Atlantic steamship line. That was part of the reason for his trip across the Atlantic.

Regular trans-Atlantic ship service had begun in 1817, with the Black Ball Packet line of sailing ships. The first steamship crossed the Atlantic in 1819, but it was not until twenty years later that steamer crossings became any more than an adventure. In 1840, aided by subsidy from the British government, Samuel Cunard began a regular steamship service between Boston and Halifax. The use of Boston, instead of New York, as the American end of the steamer line annoyed the merchants of New York. The subsidy granted the British line stirred the United States Congress into granting a similar fee to an American steamship line which would undertake to deliver the mails and maintain regular service. Cunard changed his schedule and began calling at Boston one week and New York the next. But national pride had been aroused, and from its rise came the establishment of the Collins steamship line by Edward K. Collins, of New York.

Collins went into the steamship business after a successful career in sailing ships. He had operated the Dramatic Line, which earned him a fortune in carrying service between Liverpool and New York. In 1847 he persuaded Congress to grant him a million dollars to build four steamships. Congress reasoned that if the steamers could be made available as naval ships in time of war it could justify the appropriation. And a few months later Congress also granted the Collins line an annual subsidy of nearly $400,000 for twenty voyages a year.

Edward Collins built good, fast ships for his line. He equipped them well, and in a few months they were often defeating the Cunard liners in races across the Atlantic. In 1851, Collins' *Pacific* crossed the ocean in nine days and twenty-one hours. The federal government was so well impressed that Collins' subsidy was raised to $33,000 a voyage.

Commodore Vanderbilt was not so busy planning his trip to Europe late in 1852 that he did not notice how well his compatriot in the steamship business was doing with the Atlantic run, and that there was no regular competition except from the British. Vanderbilt decided he should have a part of that business. In 1853 and 1854 Vanderbilt was too much occupied with the affairs of Accessory Transit to take more than a casual interest in trans-Atlantic shipping. In February, 1855, however, Vanderbilt proposed to the Post Office Department that he begin a semi-monthly service between New York and Liverpool alternating with the Collins line. Vanderbilt said he would do the job for $15,000 a trip—half of what Collins was getting—or $19,250 if the Post Office wanted Vanderbilt to compete with the Collins times of crossing. He also wanted a five year contract.

The Post Office was not interested. Vanderbilt steamers had a way of starting out fast and ending up slow, and the government was quite satisfied with the performance of Collins, even though his *Arctic* had been lost in a collision off Cape Race the year before, with a death toll of 322.

Vanderbilt did not get the job, but his interference did help persuade President Pierce to veto the subsidy bill for the Collins line, and it was only with the greatest of difficulty that Collins' friends in the Congress were able to have the life-giving subsidy restored.

In the summer of 1855, to further harass his rival, Vanderbilt ran a few ships across the ocean. But it was one thing to run steamers across the Atlantic during the mild summer and quite another to run through the gales and icy storms of winter, as Vanderbilt discovered that November. Vanderbilt was committed now, however, for he was building a steamship that would weigh more than five thousand tons and would cost nearly a million dollars. Thus he hoped to dazzle Congress into removing Collins' subsidy and granting it to him.

In January, 1856, Collins' *Pacific* steamed out of Liverpool harbor for New York, rode bravely into the rough Atlantic, and was never heard from again. The loss of the *Pacific* cost Collins public confidence and aroused some questions and antagonism in Congress. Vanderbilt never let up in his campaign for a moment. He was back at Congress again that spring, offering again to carry the mails to Europe at half Collins' rate, and while Congress would not abandon Collins for Vanderbilt, the objectors did manage to have Collins' subsidy cut to the $16,000 figure.

During the following year, even without subsidy, Vanderbilt opened two lines. It was not quite accurate to say he was in open competition with Collins and Cunard, for those two steamship men ran their lines in rain or sunshine, winter and summer. Vanderbilt ran only during the fair months, not during the foul ones. But he did maintain spring, summer, and fall service between New York and Bremen and between New York and Le Havre, and his huge *Vanderbilt* was the largest steamship afloat. She was also the most popular ship afloat during the fair months.

In 1858 Collins was forced into bankruptcy, partly by the heavy losses of his *Pacific,* and partly by the unpredictable and ungenerous attitudes of Congress. But Congress—or individual Congressmen at least—could not be blamed totally for the attitude taken toward Collins and other steamship men. In the original subsidy it had been stated that the steamers would also be convertible into warships. Now, late in the 1850's the southern members of Congress were contemplating the effects of the placement of all this economic and military power in northern hands. They did not like it.

Southern Senators, in particular, decided they would not support the building of more ships in northern shipyards and the subsidy of northern steamship lines.

With the failure of Collins, however, Vanderbilt did receive some of the former shipowner's subsidies, on a voyage by voyage basis. For a time he ran ships to Europe charging only eighty dollars for the first-class trip, although he charged one hundred dollars for first cabin passage in the more favored and more luxurious *Vanderbilt.* The steamer set some records, too, which Vanderbilt was proud to proclaim. On one trip in 1859 the *Vanderbilt* made the voyage from Europe in nine days, nine hours and twenty-six minutes.

Vanderbilt offered to carry the mails for the value of

the postage, and did so. He also complained constantly about the niggardliness of the federal government in not granting him subsidies. Then, on the other hand, he said time after time that he wanted nothing from the government but the right to run his ships without interference. It was sometimes hard to understand what Vanderbilt *did* want.

By the spring of 1860, however, Vanderbilt dominated the trans-Atlantic run as far as any American steam vessels were concerned. Sailing ships ran and continued to run the course, carrying much freight and some passengers. Cunard really dominated the scene, after the failure of the Collins line, for Cunard was the only trans-Atlantic steamship company offering regular service at all periods of the year. But as far as the American trade was concerned in the lessening competition of the time, Vanderbilt was the king of the Atlantic.

~ 7 ~

THE CIVIL WAR

IN 1860 COMMODORE VANDERBIILT seemed quite likely
to take over the trans-Atlantic steamship monopoly as
far as American vessels were concerned, and yet his
problems were multiplying. The British competition was
very strong. Samuel Cunard continued to receive large
subsidies from a British government which was well
aware of the importance of shipping to England's welfare.
Vanderbilt had new competition in the Screw Line,
which replaced Collins in the field.

Most important of all, Vanderbilt was now reaping a
harvest of abuse and suspicion from travelers, brought
about by years of overcrowding and dishonest practices
in passenger shipping. The dishonest practices were not
altogether Vanderbilt's fault. Standards of morality in
shipping were quite different in 1860 than they became
in the twentieth century. Vanderbilt's steamship captains
saw nothing immoral in cheating their employer as much
as possible. They did this by falsifying passenger mani-
fests. On one occasion a Vanderbilt ship that had sleeping
accommodations for five hundred passengers was found
to have put to sea with eight hundred people aboard.
The master of that ship had crammed passengers into
every nook and cranny, and, of course, the records kept

for Commodore Vanderbilt showed that the ship was completely loaded with five hundred passengers. The passage money paid by the other three hundred people went into the pockets of the captain and his purser.

If the captain did not cheat on his employer the passenger agent who booked passage and freight was almost certain to be cheating. Vanderbilt complained that his agents invariably had the best of him in their dealings. He hired two of his sons-in-law to help him with his business, but even they could not control the wrongdoing.

So the Vanderbilt ships were overloaded, undermanned, and with insufficient food aboard for the crews. By 1860 the newspapers were warning travelers that they risked life and limb in Vanderbilt ships.

Such bad publicity did not keep Vanderbilt from prospering, however, or from constantly bringing forth new schemes by which to increase his fortune. Had the times been different, he might well have begun an American-French service on a regular basis, as French business friends had suggested to him seven years before. In order to gain the favor of southern members of Congress, Vanderbilt proposed to begin a steamship line that would travel regularly between Norfolk, Virginia, and LeHavre. Such a line would bring great prestige to the South. It would make it possible, too, for southern planters and southern families to make the trip to Europe without journeying to the north. Many southerners looked with great favor on the idea.

It was brought to an untimely end, however, with the withdrawal of the southern members of Congress from Washington and the secession of the southern states, one by one, after the election of Abraham Lincoln to the Presidency in 1860. Vanderbilt, however, kept working for his plan. In November, 1860, he was still talking about it, but after the beginning of the year 1861 the southern states were going out of the Union, one by one. The plan was as dead as the Union seemed to be.

The beginning of the war, for Vanderbilt, came even before the firing on Fort Sumter by Confederate troops in Charleston harbor. On February 14, 1861, Vanderbilt's *Daniel Webster* was chartered by the War Department to carry troop reinforcements and supplies to several Union forts and outposts. One of these was Fort Jefferson in the Dry Tortugas, another was Fort Taylor at Key West. The *Daniel Webster* went from that point through the Gulf of Mexico, to deliver supplies to Port Isabel on the Brazos River in Texas.

At this time the federal government maintained very few ships other than coast guard vessels and fighting ships. Transport was a civil business, and when the army or the navy wanted men or equipment moved across the sea, they paid civilian shipowners to do the job. For the first chartering of the *Daniel Webster* Vanderbilt received $25,000. But as the war began he profited even more from the needs of the government. In October, 1861, the army chartered the Commodore's *Ocean Queen* for $2500 a day. The ship had cost the Commodore $450,000 when she was built. The army made use of her for 70 days, and when the job was done, Vanderbilt had earned $175,000—and he still had his ship, which would probably be good for at least five more years of service, even with the poor maintenance Vanderbilt devoted to wooden-hulled ships.

That same month, the Navy Department moved to send an expedition against Port Royal and Beaufort, South Carolina. This was a part of the program to blockade the Confederate coast. In April, when the war began,

President Lincoln had declared a general blockade against the whole 3500-mile coastline of the Confederacy. But declaring the coast blockaded and enforcing a blockade were two different matters, and in the beginning, the navy had very little with which to work. In the years before the Civil War the federal authorities had allowed the navy to go undermanned. The ships which had been built were outmoded, and there were far too few of them. And when the Confederacy was formed, the southerners seized control of the Norfolk navy yard with its huge store of supplies.

When war came, the navy began building ships—ironclads—as quickly as possible. It deployed as many ships as could be spared to watch the southern ports, particularly the areas accessible from the West Indies, which were to become the principal supply bases for the Confederacy. And in the summer of 1861, the navy began to move to seize bases.

First, the navy captured Fort Clark and Fort Hatteras in North Carolina, in August. The following month the Union forces took Ship Island, in the Gulf of Mexico, and the next month, the 77-ship expedition against Beaufort and Port Royal was launched.

Several of Commodore Vanderbilt's passenger vessels were used in that attack. Among them was the *Illinois*, a ship Vanderbilt had purchased from the auction of the Pacific Mail Steamship Company in 1859 for $25,000. The *Illinois* was a good sturdy vessel. She carried 750 passengers, normally, although she could carry 1200 under wartime conditions. She had cost $480,000 to build, and Vanderbilt had bought her at a "distress" price. What the war meant to Commodore Vanderbilt's fortunes was shown in the profit he made on the Port Royal expedition: He earned twice as much from that charter alone as the *Illinois* had cost him.

During the following year, Vanderbilt continued to profit from the Union's need to charter ships. He was called to Washington by Secretary of War Stanton to help the War Department plan an expedition against New Orleans. Vanderbilt met with Stanton and General Nathaniel Banks and agreed to provide the ships. Of course, he had no idea of using all his own ships in the expedition, nor did he have time to spend, personally, to inspect and evaluate every ship that was to be chartered. According to the practice of the time, he hired T. J. Southard, a shipbroker, to do that detail work.

Under a Congressional act just passed, all ships for charter were to be inspected by a naval officer and an engineer before they departed for duty. Commodore Van Brunt inspected the ships chartered by Southard for seaworthiness. Engineer Charles Haswell checked their boilers and machinery. Slowly but surely, the expedition took shape at Brooklyn Navy Yard.

The Banks expedition was to be secret, but on December 4 Commodore Vanderbilt and Mayor Opdyke of New York City boarded a navy cutter and were taken to the *North Star*, the old Vanderbilt yacht which had now become the flagship of the expedition flotilla. On board, they toasted the success of the expedition, then debarked. The soldiers sailed away to meet another flotilla which was departing from Hampton Roads, Virginia, and then to proceed against New Orleans.

From a seaman's point of view, the expedition was nearly a fiasco. The plan had been kept secret. At least the general public did not know about it, and ship captains did not know where they were headed when they set out from New York harbor that December day. Otherwise many of those old sea dogs would have refused flatly to go to sea in the ships that were given them. Some of the ships did not arrive at all. In others the soldiers risked life and limb to reach their destination. The worst case was that of the *Niagara,* whose military passengers mutinied against captain and crew before the ship was twenty-four hours out from port. They forced the captain to put in at Philadelphia.

In the military and Congressional investigations of this mutiny, it was discovered that the federal government had been thoroughly cheated in the whole charter affair. Shipbroker Southard had forced shipowners to pay him a five per cent commission of the charter rates. He had set the charter rates at about double what the shipowners were willing to accept, too.

But worst of all, Southard had chartered rotten and ill-kept ships. The ships had been overloaded, and some of them, like the *Niagara,* had been obviously unfit for the work at hand. The *Niagara*'s timbers were so rotten that they would not hold paint or a nail. She was a side-wheel vessel. She had been built for the Great Lakes trade in 1854 and was obsolete even before the war began. Yet Southard had chartered her to go out beyond Cape Hatteras in the deep Atlantic where she might founder at any moment. Commodore Vanderbilt had approved the use of the *Niagara,* although Engineer Haswell had warned him against her.

Commodore Vanderbilt was fortunate in this affair not to be pilloried by Congress for his lack of attention to duty. Others connected with the expedition were named in a Senate resolution of censure but Vanderbilt was not named, because some Senators felt he was doing enough for the Union cause to overlook this disaster.

Southard, in particular, was called upon to return the money he had collected, for in the beginning he had stated piously that he would accept no compensation for the chartering of the ships in so worthy a cause.

Vanderbilt had made no personal profit from the expedition, except in the chartering of his ships. He was not accused, then, of "shoddy" practice, although all around him in New York were people who were earning war fortunes. Vanderbilt's fortune was now becoming settled and established, and if the Vanderbilt family was still far from recognition among polite society, at least the Commodore was recognized, even with affection, by the press and people.

Although the war disturbed his tranquility and the regularity of his service, the Commodore continued to send his passenger ships to Panama in this period. He had built the first large iron-hulled steamer in the United States at the Harlan and Hollingsworth yard in Wilmington in 1859. In 1861, however, the *Champion* was no longer pride of the Vanderbilt fleet, at least with the traveling public. That summer, passengers who had traveled aboard the *Champion* complained that the meat was bad, and the rest of the food nearly inedible. No ice was to be had, even in the heat of the tropics, except by bribing a cabin boy. The dining stewards did not change the cloths on the tables until they became filthy. Sheets were not changed on the berths. The ship was badly equipped with bathrooms, and most of these facilities did not work properly. It did not even have enough spittoons!

During the next year, the Commodore again kept his merchant fleet in operation, although he was anxious to sell his ships to the government if the navy would buy them. The navy would buy a few, such as the *Daniel Webster*. That ship was chartered again in 1862 to carry troops during General McClellan's Peninsula campaign, and a few months later it was purchased outright by the U. S. Sanitary Commission to serve as a hospital ship.

The *Champion* narrowly escaped capture in December, 1862. She set out from New York with $1,350,000 in gold bullion aboard. At the same time, the famous Confederate raider *Alabama* was cruising the Atlantic and Caribbean waters, looking for rich cargoes of Union goods and for just such shipments of the gold that was so short in supply in the South.

On December 7, Vanderbilt's *Ariel* was passing Cape Maysi at the eastern end of Cuba when she saw smoke on the horizon. As the lines of the approaching vessel became clear, the captain of the *Ariel* feared that the ship bearing down on him might be one of the raiders, and he ordered full steam to try to outrun the vessel. It was commendable to try, but the superior speed of the *Alabama* made it a most unequal race. Captain Sammes of the *Alabama* had no trouble in overhauling the *Ariel*, and after he put a pair of shots across her bow the unarmed passenger ship could do nothing but stop and be boarded.

The captain, crew, and passengers of the *Ariel* fully expected to be put adrift, while the *Alabama* either sank her or took her in tow as a prize vessel to be put ashore in a neutral port and sold. But the *Alabama* was searching for bigger and more important game than the *Ariel*, and Captain Sammes acted with surprising gentleness, considering the fact that the Union blockade had been so harsh and so effective against the South. Captain Sammes confiscated all the cash and weapons aboard the *Ariel*. He disarmed 120 marines who had been traveling aboard the ship, but did not take them as prisoners of war. He forced the captain of the *Ariel* to sign a bond of $250,000 which Vanderbilt would be obliged to pay thirty days after southern independence was recognized by the Union and the war was over. Then Captain Sammes went back aboard the *Alabama*. The *Ariel* got under way, and was escorted by the Confederate warship as far as Jamaica. Luckily for Vanderbilt and the Union, the *Alabama* narrowly missed contact with the *Champion* on that voyage, for the *Champion* was carrying what she searched out on her terrorizing trips across the sea.

That year, 1862, was a busy one for the Commodore at sea. When the Confederates had taken over Norfolk Navy Yard at the beginning of the war, one of their prizes was the iron-clad hull of a vessel under construction for the Union navy—the USS *Merrimac*. The Confederate navy changed the name of the ship to the *Virginia,* and placed her on guard of the route up the James River to Richmond, capital of the Confederacy. As long as the old *Merrimac* stood guard, the Union navy could not move to capture the capital by sea.

On March 8, 1862, the *Virginia* moved out of the river into Hampton Roads, and there sank one of the Union blockaders, the *Cumberland,* set the *Congress* afire, and forced the *Minnesota* to run aground. She seemed the most fearsome ship afloat. Her armored sides protected men and machinery from the shot and shell of the Union ships. How far would she range, and how much destruction would she cause? On March 9, the *Virginia* came out of her river anchorage again to undertake the final destruction of the *Minnesota*. But the Union had brought up its desperation weapon, the ugly, awkward *Monitor,* an armored ship that looked more like a raft than a ship. The *Monitor* lay very low in the water. It was covered almost entirely by a protective sheath of iron, and its best offensive weapon was a revolving turret which could mount rapid fire against the side of the larger ship.

The *Monitor* and the *Virginia* fought a five-hour battle

that day off Hampton Roads. Neither could be said to
have won the battle outright, although the *Virginia* was
forced to return to Norfolk for repairs, nor did she come
out again to renew the battle. But Union military and
naval leaders were not sure she would not emerge one
day.

Vanderbilt was quite disappointed by the success of
the *Monitor* in keeping the *Virginia* bottled up in Norfolk harbor. He had developed a plan of his own for dealing with the ironclad, without sacrificing a Union war-
ship. He disclosed the plan to President Lincoln one
day:

Let him take his *Vanderbilt* into southern waters,
loaded inside and on the decks with bales of cotton to
stop the shells and protect the crews from the fire of the
Virginia. He would sail into Norfolk harbor no matter
how heavy the fire, ram the ironclad, and sink her. Iron-
clad or not, Vanderbilt said, the *Virginia* could not with-
stand the force of a direct ramming from the *Vanderbilt*
steaming ahead at full speed.

Lincoln did not take Vanderbilt up on this offer.
Indeed, he was so unkind as to ask Vanderbilt how much
money he would want to do this job. And later, after the
Monitor had checked the assult by the Confederate iron-
clad, the matter was forgotten. But Vanderbilt did not
forget the war, or the part he wanted to play in it. He
was far too old—nearly seventy—to fight as a soldier,
but he could give money and ships. He gave the *Vanderbilt* to the Union. He gave $100,000 on one occasion to
the Sanitary Commission to help support the treatment
of the wounded in the war.

His son, George Washington Vanderbilt, was a victim
of the Civil War, although he did not die in battle. This
young Vanderbilt had decided as a boy that he preferred

an army career to one in trade, and had secured an appointment to the United States Military Academy at West Point. George Washington Vanderbilt graduated in the class of 1860, and was commissioned a second lieutenant. At first he was posted to a fort at The Dalles, far out in the West, on the Columbia River in the new state of Oregon. Later he went into recruiting, and still later, it was reported that he served in the Corinth campaign with the Union forces.

Some time during this service George Washington Vanderbilt contracted tuberculosis, and when the doctors discovered the nature of his disease they sent him to Europe to recover, far from the turmoil of the war. There he remained until 1864 when he died on the French Riviera, victim of a disease against which even great wealth could not protect a family.

Except for his occasional efforts in behalf of the navy and his shipping charters, the Commodore behaved as did most of the businessmen of the North during the war. He continued to exert his efforts in behalf of making money. His tall, spare figure, was often seen at civic and patriotic meetings. No one could miss the Commodore. He dressed in a high white stock which had gone out of fashion at least twenty years before. Winter and summer he wore a fur-trimmed overcoat. He carried a stick with him where ever he went, and usually was to be found smoking a cigar where fire regulations permitted.

In July, 1862, Vanderbilt helped assemble a huge mass meeting at Union Square, and he sat on the platform as Mayor Opdyke and other notables urged the people of New York to do all they could to help the Union win the war. Such urging was specially needed in New York City, for before the war New York had carried on much of its trade with the South. Consequently, many New York merchants and many of their workers believed the South should be allowed to secede and go in peace. There was more pro-southern sentiment in New York City during the war than in any other northern metropolis. In fact, New York was one of the few areas in which the Democratic party, so strong in the South, maintained its power during the war.

Before the war began, the mayor of New York had been Fernando Wood, a Tammany Hall politician who lived in a mansion on Broadway near Central Park fifteen miles from the center of the city. Fernando Wood had once written to the newspapers advocating the secession of the South, and perhaps even the secession of New York City to join with the South or become a free port, at least. Such sentiments were not to be accepted by men like Vanderbilt, and soon after the war began they conducted a private fight against Wood, which resulted in his ouster from office and the election of Mayor Opdyke.

Vanderbilt here joined with W. H. Aspinwall, William B. Astor, A. T. Stewart, the merchant, and Peter Cooper, the philanthropist, to defeat Wood. Once this was accomplished these leaders worked also to defeat Governor Horatio Seymour, another Democrat, but they were not successful for Seymour was honest and capable. His enemies believed that he favored the southern cause (which was not true). An attempt was made to elect A. T. Stewart governor but it failed very badly.

Early in the 1860's the future of the shipping business began to seem very cloudy. Not only was the war hampering business, but it was apparent that transcontinental railroads were not a dream any more but a coming reality. In 1855 it became possible to travel directly from New York to Chicago by rail. By the beginning of the Civil

War rail lines ran from Chicago to New Orleans. There was not yet a road across the breadth of the continent, but railroads extended as far west as St. Joseph, Missouri, and in the far west a short line had been built near Sacramento. It was certain that within a decade at least one transcontinental railroad would be completed. If this meant nothing else to Vanderbilt, it meant the end of the California trade altogether in time. He decided, then, to spread his investments, and early in the 1860's he began investing in various railroads. Soon he became a director of the Erie Railroad.

In his sixty-ninth year Cornelius Vanderbilt, the Commodore, was ready to set out in an entirely new field and win both a fortune and a reputation that would carry him down in history. Had Vanderbilt ended his career in 1863, before he went into railroading seriously, he would be remembered by few men.

His principal competitor of the steamboat period was "Liveoak" George Law, another Commodore and multimillionaire. Law was so well known that in 1856 he was nominated for President and had a considerable backing, particularly in Pennsylvania. Law built the mighty *Oregon*. He built the high bridge that brought fresh water down to New York City from the Croton reservoir across the Harlem River. He built and operated the United States Mail Steamship Company. He competed with Vanderbilt in the Staten Island ferry business and later bought some of Vanderbilt's holdings. He took over and salvaged the New York street railway business. Yet fifty years after his death few Americans knew the name of George Law, and fewer yet knew any details of his story. It is one matter to attain fame in the world, but quite another to have it transmitted into history. And in 1863, although Commodore Vanderbilt was almost a legendary character within his own family, he had not yet begun to rise to his full stature.

Still, he was wealthy enough and famous enough that the fiftieth anniversary of his wedding to Sophia created a considerable stir. The family gathered, one hundred fifty strong, at the Commodore's house on Washington Place, across from the old cemetery which had once been the Potter's Field of New York. This was the edge of Greenwich Village, an area that had been far above the northern limits of New York City when the Commodore first came to New York, but was now in the heart of the city. Brothers, sisters, children, grandchildren, and great grandchildren all were there. They came up the steps and into the parlor of the house, where a huge family tree had been erected, bearing the names of all the children, with Sophia and the Commodore listed at the top. The party was entertained by a brass band, and by members of the family who sang. Other children made speeches. The room was decorated by a bust of the Commodore on one side and a statue of Wilhelm Tell's son on the other. The Commodore gave Sophia a two-foot gold music box which was a copy of his ship the *Roanoke*. She gave him a gold model of a house. The family sang and talked and danced until ten o'clock, then ate a huge supper, and then sang and celebrated until midnight, when the band played "Home Sweet Home," and the party ended.

This display of family togetherness was not altogether an accurate picture of Vanderbilt's home life, however. The one greatest disappointment in the Commodore's life was the character of his sons. His eldest son, William Henry Vanderbilt, was a heavy-set stolid man in his early forties. William Henry had been a clerk in the financial house of Daniel Drew before his health broke down and he had been forced to move back to Staten Island and become a farmer. For years the Commodore had almost ignored William Henry. The boy had gone his own way and had made his farm one of the more prosperous on the island. This year, 1863, he began to redeem himself in his father's eyes a little by salvaging the Staten Island Railroad.

That chain of events came about quite naturally. As the richest citizen of Staten Island, Vanderbilt had purchased much property there over the years. He had become involved in a number of businesses. Sometimes he did this to make profits, and sometimes he did it to help friends and relatives. At any rate, by 1863 he was involved in the Staten Island Railroad. Five years before, the railroad became insolvent and went into the hands of receivers. The stock of the railroad was literally worth nothing at all.

William Henry Vanderbilt offered to try to rehabilitate the line if his father would back him. Vanderbilt begrudgingly gave his eldest son this chance, and William Henry surprised him by turning the Staten Island line into a profitable road.

The Commodore was less fortunate in his other sons. George lay dying on the Riviera, unable even to come home for the important golden wedding celebration. Cornelius Jeremiah, the second son, was the most burdensome of all to the Commodore, for Cornelius Jeremiah was an epileptic and an extremely weak character. From the days of his boyhood he had been in constant trouble, not due to his disease but due to his character. The disease was one which doctors of that day did not understand at all. Epilepsy was diagnosed as a kind of insanity, and

Cornelius Jeremiah therefore spent much of his youth in insane asylums or under the watchful eyes of a number of doctors.

During the early days of the California gold rush, Cornelius Jeremiah had shipped aboard a sailing vessel as a seaman, bound for Cape Horn and California. But he had fallen ill on the trip and proved of no use on the ship. He was stranded in California by a disgusted captain, and then he cashed a draft on his father without permission.

That was a common practice of Cornelius Jeremiah. In those days, before the telegraph, men of good reputation were able to cash drafts in their family name, or even on friends. A man's word was his bond. If he cashed a draft and then the person on whom it was drawn refused to honor it, the man who cashed it might go to prison. Certainly he would be ruined.

Cornelius Jeremiah cashed sight drafts on his father in California, in Washington, D.C., and elsewhere. Sometimes he was thrown into jail, when his father refused to honor them. But always in the end the Commodore relented and paid.

Now, as the war was drawing to an end, Cornelius Jeremiah thought of a scheme that would help him gain a fortune in his own right. He planned to go to New Orleans, which was in Union hands, and use good Union money to buy huge quantities of cotton, which he would buy cheaply on a depressed market, and then sell at high prices in the North where it was needed.

The trouble was that Cornelius Jeremiah borrowed money to go there in the beginning, spent it and lost it at the gambling table, and borrowed more. Finally he wrote a draft on Horace Greeley, editor of the *Tribune,* who had befriended him, and managed to get enough money to come home. The plan had come to nothing. Cornelius Jeremiah had none of the luck of his father, for as Cornelius Jeremiah came home empty handed, the Commodore was in the midst of the greatest financial coup in his life and the most significant business undertaking he had ever considered. Vanderbilt was beginning the consolidation of a handful of tiny railways into what would become the most important freight and passenger system in the country. He was beginning work to put together the New York Central Railroad System.

~ 8 ~

THE NEW YORK CENTRAL

COMMODORE VANDERBILT had been interested in railroads for many years before he became seriously interested in owning and running one of his own. In the beginning his interest was aroused because railroads connected with his steamboats in New Jersey, on the Hudson River, and on Long Island Sound. By gaining influence over a railroad, through stock ownership, Vanderbilt was able to press the railroad managements to use Vanderbilt steamers for their connecting links.

He did this successfully in Long Island, and he tried to do it elsewhere. He and Daniel Drew finally bought control of the Stonington rail line in order to make sure that they could control the traffic from the end of the line to New York.

Thereafter Vanderbilt had invested in a number of railroads especially in New York, New Jersey, and Pennsylvania. These investments were not made to control the rail lines, but in hope for income and capital increase and in playing the old Wall Street game of stock speculation. During these years of the 1830's, 1840's, and 1850's Vanderbilt was a steamboat man, but as he gained capital that he did not need in his business, he put it into investments that would yield high return. In those days railroads were the greatest gamble on the stock market.

Vanderbilt's greater interest in railroads began in the early 1860's when he found himself hampered in his steamer enterprises. Later in life he was to say that he had never really thought about becoming a railroad man when he began investing in rail stock, but had done so only to make money.

In 1863 Vanderbilt became seriously interested in the New York and Harlem Railroad, one of the first to be granted a franchise to operate in New York State. The Harlem had been put together thirty years before but it had not prospered in recent years. Its originators had proposed to run locomotives through the city. In fact, the railroad was organized in 1831 to take passengers and freight from New York City, on the lower end of Man hattan Island, through the country farmland to Harlem, on the upper end of the island. In the beginning locomotives ran from the end of the island all the way. Then two locomotives blew up and another burned right in the center of New York. The city council banned locomotives below Fourteenth Street. Thereafter the Harlem's trains ran only to the edge of the city by locomotive, and were drawn by horses into the city. Eventually, although the railroad charter gave the Harlem the right to operate in New York, the railroad abandoned many of the horsecars.

In 1830 the population of New York City was 200,000, but thirty years later it was more than twice as large. The population increase had brought the city far north of Fourteenth Street. The Harlem Railroad had fallen on disastrous days however, for the Hudson River line had gained the right to run up the Hudson River, and the Harlem was forced to wander inland and seek a more devious route before turning toward the state capital at

Albany. The Hudson River line had been backed by John Jacob Astor and others. They had simply outmaneuvered the Harlem, and the growth of the city and the area had worked in their favor. Consequently, in 1863 the Harlem line was run down and its stock on Wall Street had fallen from par to nine dollars a share.

At that bargain price Commodore Vanderbilt began to buy Harlem stock. For, like John Jacob Astor, the Commodore saw that the city was continuing to move northward, and as it moved, the transportation system must be expanded to keep pace with it. The Harlem line might not have much traffic, but it did have one great attribute: an original franchise which permitted it to come into the city and operate trains. No other line had such a guarantee from the state and city governments. The problem of the Harlem was that its geography was all wrong, and because of that, the line had no money with which to expand its system inside the city.

Vanderbilt was not the only businessman who saw opportunity in the need for mass transportation in New York City. George Law had noted the need even earlier and had begun to lay his plans. Law went to the state legislature at Albany and there secured a new franchise to operate street railways for his Consolidated Stage Company within the city of New York. But at that same time, Commodore Vanderbilt sought approval of Mayor Opdyke and the New York Common Council for his plan. He received that approval, but that did not yet establish Vanderbilt's rights. Before the approval could become law, it had to be accepted by the superior Board of Councilmen, and the Law claim had to be settled.

The governor vetoed the bill which gave George Law the right to lay tracks in New York. That solved one problem. Now it remained necessary for Vanderbilt to persuade the Councilmen that his proposal was in the best interests of the city.

Already there was some confusion in the air. When the Common Council accepted Vanderbilt's plan, he immediately sent workmen out to start tearing up the streets and laying track. When the legislature accepted Law's plan, the Consolidated Stage Company did the same, until Governor Horatio Seymour vetoed the bill.

The destruction of the cobblestones was ended by injunction for the moment, but the Councilmen still had to act on Vanderbilt's proposal. Unfortunately, New York's legislators in state and city were not above taking bribes or passing laws which would lead to profit for themselves. And on this occasion the Commodore's old acquaintance and business associate Daniel Drew saw how he could turn the Vanderbilt maneuver into profit for himself and for the Councilmen.

Drew was a member of the board of directors of the Harlem Railroad. Consequently, although Commodore Vanderbilt was elected president of the railroad that year, Drew knew the railroad's plans. He also was well aware of the heavy fluctuation in Harlem stock on Wall Street, because for years he had maintained his investment house there to speculate in the quick rise and fall of stocks.

There were two ways of speculating in stock. One way was to become a "bull"—which meant that the investor wagered his money on the rise of the stock. For example, if a stock started at 100, the "bulls" who believed there was some reason for the stock to rise, would buy at that figure. If they were right, the stock might rise to 150 in a few days. Then the "bulls" would sell their stock and clear a profit of fifty cents on every dollar invested. Actually they would clear far more than that, because to buy stocks a man needed to put down only ten or fifteen per cent of the value of the stock. The only danger in buying this way—on margin—was if the stock *declined* in value. Then the person who had bought the stock without putting up all the money would be forced to find the rest of the money or go bankrupt. In other words, if a "bull" bought a stock at 100, putting down $15, and, instead of rising, the stock fell to 50, then the "bull" would want to sell, because he was afraid the stock might go even lower. However, he would have to put up the other $35, which he had lost, to make the value of $100.

That was how Vanderbilt was playing the market in these days. He was always a "bull," always betting on the increase in values that he could bring about by actions of his own. His secret was to invest heavily only in businesses that he controlled in one way or another. In that way he was not at the mercy of some other managers. Now, he was investing in Harlem Railroad stock, and by securing his own election as president of the company, he made sure that he would make the decisions about the future of the line.

Having bought a great amount of stock at $9 a share, the Commodore was very pleased to see that his plan for the street railroad system brought the stock up steadily. It went to $48, then up to $72.

Daniel Drew watched this phenomenal rise with interest. He was shrewd enough to realize that the only thing that had changed with the Harlem Railroad was the movement led by Vanderbilt to secure the right to run trains into New York City proper. If that right were withheld by the city council, the Harlem Railroad would be in the same position it had been before. It would again be a struggling little line running crazily out into the heart of Westchester county, and then straggling its way north to Chatham. Nothing would have changed, and the railroad's stock would undoubtedly find its way back down to a figure around $9 a share where it had stood before Vanderbilt came forth with his plan for expansion.

Since Vanderbilt proposed to make his fortune by playing the market as a "bull," Drew shrewdly thought he could confound Vanderbilt and make a fortune for himself by speculating in the second manner common to Wall Street. Drew decided to become a "bear." He would wager that the stock of the Harlem Railroad would go down, not up.

The way to do this was to take up a practice which in Wall Street was and is called "selling short." When a stock speculator "sells short" at 100, that means that he bets that the stock will fall somewhere below $100 a share. He does not put up any money at the time, but he tells a broker that he will guarantee to deliver a share on a specified day. The other person says he will pay $100 for the share on that day.

For example: on June 15, a "short seller" sold a share of stock for $100, and promised that he would deliver it on September 1. The buyer agreed to pay $100 a share at that time. The seller did not really own the stock at all. He had just agreed to deliver a share at $100 three months later. If the price fell to $50 on September 1, all the "short seller" had to do was go out and buy a share at that price, then deliver it to the man who had agreed to buy the stock at $100. The "short seller" then made a profit of $50 without putting up any money at all. The danger in "shortselling" was if the price of the stock rose in the three-month period. If it rose from $100 a share to $150, on September 1, the "short seller" would have to buy a share of stock at $150—and sell it to the person he had promised it to for $100. The "short seller" then lost $50 a share, and if he could not deliver stock to those he promised, he would go bankrupt and might go to prison for fraud.

When Daniel Drew decided to sell Harlem stock short, he embarked on a plan as complex as that of Vanderbilt. The difference was that Vanderbilt's plan involved the improvement of the railroad. Drew's plan involved the destruction of Vanderbilt's plan.

Drew quietly began to talk to the men who sat on New York City's Board of Councilmen. He showed them how they could all make their own fortunes. All they had to do was agree to cancel the permission granted to the Harlem Railroad, but pretend for a few weeks that they would pass on the idea. While they were pretending to approve of the franchise each councilman could "sell short" in Harlem Railroad stock. The councilmen would not have to put up actual cash. All they had to do was promise to deliver the stock later at the price prevailing on the day of their transaction. So it seemed simple. The councilmen would "sell short," without putting up money, and then when they canceled the franchise, they would go out and buy stock and deliver it. After they canceled the franchise, the stock would fall quickly. They could buy it up cheaply, and deliver it at prices set when the franchise seemed to be going through.

It was an almost foolproof plan. Drew did not see how they could lose.

So in May, 1863, Daniel Drew and the councilmen began "selling short" in Harlem Railroad stock, all the time pretending that it was certain that the right to bring trains into New York would be granted to the railroad.

Vanderbilt worked at his plans for improving the Harlem. Wall Street brokers watched him. Investors watched him. And they took confidence and began buying stock, and making arrangements with the "short sellers" to deliver stock at future dates. The price was 72. It rose steadily, to 80, then to 90, to 100, and to 110. The councilmen and Daniel Drew decided that the figure of $110 per share was as high as they ought to go. They could not delay much longer, lest their secret escape.

On June 25 the councilmen canceled the franchise. Then they sat back and waited for the stock to fall in value.

Immediately Harlem stock dropped to 72 points. The councilmen who had "sold short" at $110 were sure they had earned their fortunes right then. All they had to do was buy stock, that day, at $72 a share. When it came time to deliver the stock to the person who had promised to buy it at $110 a share, the "short seller" would clear $38 profit on each share.

But there were two factors which the councilmen and Daniel Drew had forgotten. First, in their excessive greed, the "short sellers" had made contracts which involved more Harlem Railroad stock than had ever been issued. Second, when the councilmen vetoed the railroad franchise, Commodore Vanderbilt was quick to realize what had happened. He began to buy up the "short sale" contracts as quickly as he could, and to buy all the Harlem stock he could find on the Wall Street market.

So while Harlem stock dropped to 72 on June 26, by June 27 it had risen twenty-five points to 97, and as Vanderbilt kept buying the stock kept rising. The "short sellers" searched the market, trying to find stock for sale, but they could find none. Vanderbilt and his friends were buying every available share.

All summer long the "short sellers" scoured the market and watched with anguish while the price of Harlem Railroad stock went higher and higher. Finally, in August, the price of Harlem stock went to $180 a share, and Vanderbilt and his friends consented to let the "bears" buy stock at that figure to fulfill their contracts.

Vanderbilt did not succeed in getting the street railway franchise for the Harlem Railroad, but he did make a fortune of millions of dollars on the speculation. Daniel Drew and the councilmen lost millions.

One great difference between Vanderbilt and Daniel Drew was in their whole approach to business. Had Daniel Drew just earned a fortune in Harlem stock, he would have sold out his whole interest and begun speculating in something else. Vanderbilt, however, took a good look at the situation of the Harlem Railroad, even though it was in no better position after the franchise refusal than it had been a few months before when the stock was selling at $9 a share. Unless something were done, obviously, the stock would begin to drop again down to some point around $9.

His first move was to travel to Albany to try to reason with the legislators there. He carried with him a satchel full of greenbacks, because he had learned earlier that money possessed the greatest reasoning power of all for the legislators. He passed his money around lavishly, and came back to New York confident that the legislature would now give the Harlem road the franchise that the city of New York had denied him.

When Daniel Drew heard that Vanderbilt had gone to Albany, he went to the capital himself, with even more money, and the same promise to the legislators—that they could make their fortunes by selling Harlem short. No one would suspect that any speculators would try the game so quickly after it had failed before. All the legislators had to do now was to assure Vanderbilt that his plan would be accepted, and then finally reject it.

Vanderbilt heard of the maneuver. He called together

his friends and supporters, and persuaded them to try to buy up every single share of Harlem stock on the market. As the "short sellers" made their contracts, so did Vanderbilt and his friends buy up all the stock—cornered it, they said. On March 16, 1864, the Harlem stock was selling at $149, and Wall Street was ablaze with rumors of Vanderbilt's plans for the road after the legislature approved the franchise. On that day, on schedule, the legislators threw out Vanderbilt's plan and the stock began, slowly, to sink. Vanderbilt and his friends had been buying quietly. Now they threw caution to the winds and bought with all the resources at their disposal. In a few weeks they had bought so heavily that on paper they owned 27,000 more shares of Harlem Railroad stock than existed. That meant they could control the price of the stock at will, for they had almost all of it in their safes. If the "short sellers" wanted to deliver stock—they had to buy from Vanderbilt.

Vanderbilt was so angry with the legislators for taking his bribes and then turning on him that he wanted to put the price of the stock up to $1000 a share and thus bankrupt every one of them. But friends persuaded him that if he did that, he would also bankrupt half the financial houses on Wall Street, and might even cause a national panic. That would not be in Vanderbilt's interest, he realized, so he allowed himself to be persuaded to let stock be sold at $285 a share. Most of the legislators were bankrupt by this, but the financial houses which had guessed wrong were only crippled. They could survive.

The two cornerings of Harlem Railroad stock still had not solved the Commodore's problem of how to make the railroad operate profitably, however. But now Vanderbilt did devise a program.

It was an important decision, because it involved a great change in the Commodore's life. He decided to leave the steamship business and concentrate all his efforts and wealth on railroads.

This year, 1864, Commodore Vanderbilt sold most of his steamships for $3,000,000 and invested the majority of his capital in two railroads. He was already heavily invested in the Harlem, but to this he added the control of the Hudson River Railroad, which had the enviable right of running up the east bank of the Hudson as far as Greenbush, the town opposite Albany on the river.

Vanderbilt's decision to invest his money in the Hudson Railroad at this time was not made by guess but by very shrewd reasoning. The Harlem's principal attraction to him in the beginning had been its right to enter New York City. Further, the Harlem had a spur line which connected it to the Hudson. By putting the two railroads together, Vanderbilt could bring all freight and all passengers into a single railroad station, thus cutting his expenses in many ways and making the two lines far more valuable than either of them might have been separately.

The Commodore had another plan in mind even at that time. He wanted to connect the Hudson and Harlem lines with still another railroad, the New York Central. The Central was an amalgamation of a number of small railroads which ran from Albany to Buffalo on Lake Erie. It was owned by a number of wealthy New York businessmen, including the Astor family, and in the beginning, while Vanderbilt was able to buy some stock, he was not able to secure any large interest in the road. It did not seem that it would be possible for him to combine all these railroads, until one of the millionaire owners died and the closely held stock became available on the open market.

Quietly, Vanderbilt kept on buying all the stock he could purchase in the New York Central. While he could not acquire control, shortly after the end of the Civil War he did secure enough stock to obtain election of his son-in-law, H. F. Clark, as a director of the line. That same year Clark managed to persuade the other directors of the Central to grant a $100,000 bonus every year to the Hudson River line, for the privilege of shipping goods and passengers. The Central had used the Hudson line only during the winter months for transshipment. In the good weather, Central passengers and freight were loaded aboard the steamers of Daniel Drew's People's Steamboat line, which offered cheaper passage than Vanderbilt's railroad. In the winter, however, the Hudson was frozen over, and the Central proprietors had always used the Hudson River Railroad.

Vanderbilt was quite pleased with this new arrangement with the Central, but it did not last long. The major stockholders of the Central line erupted in anger when they learned of the $100,000 bonus and transshipment arrangement with Vanderbilt. Who had authorized it, they asked? Why had it been done? In a fiery meeting late in 1866, the stockholders ousted the management of the Central railroad and threw out all the agreements with Vanderbilt.

Here the New York Central stockholders made a serious mistake. Had they made such a change in the spring or summer, they would not have been so vulnerable. But by making the change in the winter, they put themselves at Vanderbilt's mercy. A few weeks after he had been so rousingly defeated in Albany, Vanderbilt struck back. He announced that from then on the Hudson River Railroad would not accept any transshipment of passengers or freight from the New York Central line. In other words, if a passenger wanted to travel from Buffalo to

New York City by way of the New York Central, he would have to get off the train at Albany, make his way by ferry across the Hudson River, taking care of his own baggage all the while, and then buy tickets on the Hudson River line at Greenbush. It was a great deal of trouble for passengers, obviously, and even more trouble for freight shippers. Vanderbilt pointed out, too, that the only way to go from Buffalo to New York City without such transfer would be to use the Erie Railroad, in which he was also buying stock at that time.

The New York Central management held out for five days. It was obvious that if Vanderbilt stuck to his guns, the Central would be ruined before spring thaws would make it possible to use the river boats again. To be sure, the New York legislature began an investigation into the situation, but legislative investigations took time. Every day the Hudson River embargo continued the Central would be pushed closer to disaster.

On January 19 the Central management capitulated. Within a year Commodore Vanderbilt had acquired a controlling interest in the New York Railroad, and just a year after the argument with the Central he became president of that railroad, too. All that was left was to consolidate the three railroads in name as he had already done in fact. Thereafter, for the first time, one railroad ran from Buffalo to Albany to New York City, serving the great industrial and farm market of New York State, and giving New York direct access to the inland shipping and transport of Lake Erie. It was an important move in the development of America.

~9~

THE ERIE FIGHT

After he had gained control of the New York Central System, Commodore Vanderbilt continued to invest in railroads. He claimed, of course, that he had not the slightest intention of taking control of any of them, but his actions in connection with the Erie Railroad aroused suspicion among some citizens.

The Erie line was built by foresighted men before Vanderbilt had taken control of the three railroads that he built into his system. The Erie connected New York City with Lake Erie also, on a direct route from Buffalo that did not serve the state capital at Albany and then come down the Hudson as Vanderbilt's lines did. Still, by virtue of its route to Buffalo the Erie was Vanderbilt's single great competitor at this time. Like other businessmen of his day, the Commodore had great regard for monopoly. He felt, in fact, that monopoly was the sensible way to do business when it was possible to build such an empire.

Why, then, would Commodore Vanderbilt deny any intention of taking over the Erie Railroad and putting it together with his other lines? The answer lies in the story of Commodore Vanderbilt's great adventure with Daniel Drew, Jim Fisk, and Jay Gould in the settlement of the future of the Erie line.

Daniel Drew was just a few years younger than Commodore Vanderbilt, and yet in many ways he seemed older, more cranky, and worse-tempered than the Commodore. One thing was sure—while the Commodore and Daniel Drew shared admiration for money and power, their ways of getting it were as different as night and day. In his later years Vanderbilt seemed to grow a shade more mellow than in the past. Daniel Drew seemed only to grow more hypocritical. He was still the same man who had watered the cattle he had first salted and then sold to a German butcher, Henry Astor. As the years rolled by Drew grew thinner and more cadaverous. He wore black clothing and carried an enormous watch. He slept with all the windows locked and the heat turned up high. He spent night after night fingering his book of prayer, and he became a deacon in the Methodist Episcopal church. He was also inclined to bouts of solitary drunkenness.

During the Civil War years, Daniel Drew had taken a young man named James Fisk, Jr. into his financial house. Fisk was a fat young man. He looked slow on his feet. But in fact he proved even quicker when money was flashed before him than Daniel Drew had proved in finding ways of taking it away from any man who was so careless as to show it. Jim Fisk was in his early thirties at the end of the Civil War. He had worked for the Boston department store of Jordan-Marsh Company and as a securities dealer before he met Daniel Drew. Drew backed Fisk in a brokerage house, and the pair began to negotiate financial deals with railroads, steamship lines, and stock issues. By 1867 Fisk had grown so slick that even Daniel Drew was a little bit afraid of him, and rightly so.

Drew also joined in partnership from time to time

with Jay Gould, as light-fingered a citizen as ever watered
the stock of a railroad. Gould had been born a farm boy
in upstate New York, like Drew. One of his first business
deals was to cheat his employer out of a piece of land.
Gould had a job in a general store, and one day he heard
his employer talking about buying a specific plot of land.
Gould borrowed some money from his family and bought
the land himself. And when the storekeeper wanted to
buy it, he discovered that his clerk now owned it and
wanted twice as much money as the previous owner.
Gould got his price and lost his job. He felt it was worth
it. His course in life was set. He was inevitably headed
for the big city of New York and the speculative market
place of Wall Street.

By 1867, Drew, Fisk, and Gould were all directors of
the Erie Railroad. Drew had tried his short-selling maneuver in the Erie and had succeeded in making a fortune
of more than two million dollars by doing it. He had,
however, angered a number of Erie stockholders to the
point of action. They asked Vanderbilt to step in and
help them. For a time it seemed that the Commodore
might do just that, but then he turned around and helped
Daniel Drew instead. Some thought he had made a deal
with the Erie for future consolidation.

Vanderbilt seemed to think so too. At least in the
following year when he approached Drew and company
with such an idea, he was shocked when they turned him
down. In February, 1868, the Commodore declared open
war on Daniel Drew and his two cronies in the Erie.

The war started with a legal maneuver. The Commodore had a representative on the Erie board of directors
at this time. This man appeared before Judge Barnard
of the New York Supreme Court to get an injunction
which would forbid the railroad to pay Drew either inter-

est or principal on a loan he had made. The reason for this action was obscure, but the real reason for Vanderbilt's anger was a report that Drew and his friends were planning to link the Erie to Chicago.

Since Vanderbilt had recently acquired the Michigan Southern Railroad, which gave him access to Chicago through the New York Central, the Commodore did not take kindly to this report. He felt it was time to eliminate such untrustworthy rivals from his sphere of influence.

The next day Vanderbilt's man came before the same judge and petitioned that Daniel Drew be suspended as a director of the Erie for wrongdoing. Drew had purchased a small and virtually worthless railroad called the Buffalo, Bradford & Pittsburgh for about a quarter of a million dollars. He had turned around and *leased* it to the Erie for three million dollars, payable in convertible bonds. Those convertible bonds were later to play an important part in the Erie fight, for the word "convertible" meant that under certain conditions the bonds could be converted into stock. The basic condition that would have to be met was the agreement of the board of directors and the management. At the moment, Daniel Drew, Jim Fisk, and Jay Gould seemed to have the Erie in their pocket. That was why Commodore Vanderbilt petitioned Judge Barnard to have Drew removed.

Drew was not removed immediately, however, and while Vanderbilt was maneuvering, so was the triumvirate of Drew, Fisk, and Gould. On the day following Vanderbilt's legal attempt to remove Drew, the three secured authorization of the majority of the board to take $10,000,000 in convertible bonds in addition to Drew's holdings. The three said they were taking the bonds to cover the cost of track improvement and to build a new depot for the Erie. The Commodore did not believe

Cornelius Vanderbilt. An engraving by A. H. Ritchie, about 1865.

Portrait of Phebe Hand Vanderbilt, the Commodore's mother, by Weart Banta. About 1835.

Vanderbilt's boyhood home in Stapleton, Staten Island.

THE PEOPLE VERSUS MONOPOLY.

"The People versus Monopoly." Caricature depicting Commodore Vanderbilt and the Hudson River steamboat competition. About 1840.

The steamer NORTH STAR stranded on the beach at Planas Island on the Panama route. From a woodcut in the *New York Illustrated News*, 1859.

U. S. War Steamship VANDERBILT in chase of the pirate ALABAMA. The Commodore's largest steamship equipped with guns as a naval auxiliary in the Civil War. Woodcut from *Harper's Weekly*, 1862.

"The Statue Unveiled or The Colossus of Roads." Currier & Ives Print, about 1869.

"Fast Trotters on Harlem Lane." Commodore Vanderbilt is third from left in the foreground. A Currier & Ives lithograph of 1870.

New York Stock Exchange,

Located at No. 10 Broad street.

The New York Stock Exchange at 10 Broad Street, New York, N. Y., in the year of the "Panic" of 1873.

them. He went back to court and obtained another injunction against the conversion of any bonds into stock.

Having done so much, the Commodore then began buying Erie stock, as he had bought Harlem stock in previous encounters with Drew and his friends. There was a difference this time, however. In past fights with Drew, Vanderbilt had always been in control of the railroad in question. This time the three wily speculators were in control.

"If the printing press don't break down," said Jim Fisk, talking about the Commodore's attempt to buy all the stock of the Erie, "we'll give the old hog all he wants."

On March 7, the conspirators were ready to swing into action. March 7 was a Saturday. The Stock Exchange would be closed the following day and would reopen on Monday morning. Drew, Fisk, and Gould had more than 36 hours in which to complete their plans.

In spite of the court ruling that no bonds could be converted into stock, the three speculators seized control of the railroad's stock books. Then they began transferring bonds into stock, and made arrangements with a printer to print up new stock certificates.

On Monday morning, as Wall Street firms began opening their doors and the Exchange made ready for business, Commodore Vanderbilt ordered his brokers to begin buying Erie. It was apparent that he intended to corner the market and seize control of that railroad to add to his holdings. But this morning, there were 100,000 new shares of stock on the market, the ink hardly dry. Vanderbilt did not know it. No one knew it except Drew, Fisk, Gould and a printer who did not care.

Vanderbilt's brokers bought all day long. The price rose from eighty to eighty-three dollars a share for Erie that day. But the next day, an entirely new batch of stock was thrown on the market. Wall Street began to under stand that something was not as it ought to be.

That following day Erie dropped to seventy-eight dollars a share, and became more shaky as the market closed. Vanderbilt had failed! He had not cornered the market, and he had lost $7,000,000 in his attempt.

Within a few hours Vanderbilt learned the true state of affairs. Drew, Fisk, and Gould were frightened enough of the Commodore and the law that they fled to Jersey City that night. Jersey City was outside the jurisdiction of New York State courts: By moving across the Hudson they hoped to avoid prosecution for violation of the court order. They opened their offices at Taylor's Hotel, and Jim Fisk brought along his lady friend, Josie Mansfield, an actress. The three set up headquarters at Taylor's Hotel, and asked for police protection against an attempt by Vanderbilt to abduct them.

Immediately, however, the three speculators began to fall out among themselves. All of them were afraid of the Commodore's wrath, and all of them knew that he would never rest as long as he was injured in the pocket-book. They could not hope to return to New York as long as Judge Barnard held the injunction against them. Having violated the injunction, they were subject to heavy fines and imprisonment, and even to charges of outright fraud—which of course they had committed.

Simultaneously, the three began individual and secret negotiatons with Commodore Vanderbilt and an attempt to bribe the New York State legislature into legalizing their illegal acts by passing a new law governing the stock issues of the Erie Railroad.

Each night one or the other of the three conspirators would sneak across the Hudson, without telling his friends, and would make his way to 10 Washington Place, where Vanderbilt lived. Night after night, Vanderbilt would talk and argue. His terms were simple. He wanted his money back. If he did not get it, he would not relent.

The three speculators did win one temporary victory, through their influence on a judge in Albany and through Boss Tweed, who was just then assuming power as chief of Tammany and the greatest rogue in the history of New York City.

For several years Boss Tweed had been planning to seize control of New York City and to milk its funds into his own pocket and the pockets of his friends. He was serving as a State Senator, and in Albany he got to know most of the other members of the legislature. It was not long before he had the others eating out of his hand. From time to time Vanderbilt had pressed money on Tweed to accomplish certain aims. Tweed had distributed part of the money to his trusted legislators and had kept part of it, and Vanderbilt's laws had usually passed without trouble.

On this occasion, however, Jay Gould went to Albany with two million dollars in currency which he was willing to spend to persuade the legislators to legalize the Erie stock funds. Vanderbilt wanted Judge Barnard made receiver of the Erie Railroad during the period of confusion and trouble. No one knew what the stock status of the road truly was at this point, and until its affairs could be straightened out it was to be placed in the hands of a third party, who could prevent further raiding of the company's treasury.

Gould managed to have the appointment of Judge Barnard thrown out. Then the Commodore had his son-in-law appointed. Gould managed to have that reversed, and finally he was so successful as to secure the appointment of Peter Sweeny, a hireling of Boss Tweed, as the receiver for the railroad.

Separately, Boss Tweed agreed to go to work for Gould, Fisk, and Drew, for a consideration.

At first the legislators seemed to be leaning towards Vanderbilt's position. Then they leaned toward Gould. But in the meantime in New York City the negotiations continued.

On March 27, the legislature finally decided in favor of Vanderbilt. The Erie bill, which would have legalized the actions of the three conspirators, was voted down. Gould was arrested a few days later on the contempt charges and had to post a bond of $500,000. He just happened to have the $500,000.

But in New York City, negotiations were suddenly beginning to bear fruit. The triumvirate, negotiating separately, had begun to realize that Vanderbilt meant business, and that they could never do business in New York, nor could the affairs of the Erie be settled, until they settled with him first. Fisk and Gould proceeded to do that, skinning poor old Daniel Drew in the process and taking most of what they had to relinquish out of Drew's holdings.

The conspirators gave Vanderbilt back most of his money, and he gave back the stock, which had now dropped to a value of $40 per share. Daniel Drew was forced to resign as treasurer of the company, and to return a half million dollars he had taken from the company's funds.

Then, on April 20, all opposition to the Erie Bill suddenly evaporated in Albany and the bill was passed. Judge Barnard called the lawbreakers before him and began issuing fines of only $10 to settle that part of the affair. In the end, Gould and Fisk retained control of the Erie, and Daniel Drew was forced out altogether. His affairs then went downhill rapidly, and a few years later the old man died broke. When he was found dead in a tiny room of a hotel, his personal possessions—all he had in the world—came to a value of less than $500.

Commodore Vanderbilt was really less concerned about the million dollars or so he had lost in the Erie fight than one might expect him to have been, but there was a good reason for his lightheartedness. That year he took a trick out of old Daniel Drew's bag and applied it to railroads. Where Daniel Drew had brought skinny cows to market fattened for a few hours on salt and water, Vanderbilt diluted the stock of his railroads with millions of dollars worth of water.

Vanderbilt first watered the Hudson River line by adding three and a half millions of dollars worth of stock to the railroad, without putting up any more money. Then he declared a stock dividend for himself of twenty-three million dollars on the New York Central line.

Having so increased his own capital position, Vander bilt turned his attention once again to Jim Fisk and Jay Gould. He was not really satisfied to let them get away with the victory they had won—at least partly—in the Erie fight. Vanderbilt was never satisfied with anything less than total victory for himself. So he declared a rate war on the Erie road in that competing area where they operated—between New York and Buffalo. Freight and passenger rates both fell. Finally, Vanderbilt cut the rate for a carload of cattle from $160 to $40. Gould and Fisk cut back. Vanderbilt dropped the rate again. Gould and Risk responded in kind. Exasperated, Vanderbilt cut the freight rate to $1 a carload for shipping. Then Fisk and Gould pulled a theatrical coup which startled Wall Street but also caused all the financial men of New York to dissolve in laughter. Fisk and Gould secretly went to Buffalo, dealt with drovers there, and bought up six thousand head of cattle. Carefully, they made arrangements with a third party, who then shipped the cattle over the New York Central and delivered them to this worthy pair at the other end. Then they let the world know that they had outfoxed the old Commodore by using his railroad at $1 a carload to make a huge profit on cattle sales.

"Never kick a skunk," Vanderbilt growled, as he admitted himself defeated by these scoundrels and withdrew from the rate war.

Following the Erie fight, Vanderbilt and his son William Henry concentrated on building up the New York Central System. The New York legislature would not allow them to consolidate the lines at first into one system, but that did not make too much difference, because Vanderbilt ran his three railroads as though they were one. Then, when he acquired the Lake Shore & Michigan Southern and the Michigan Central, he extended his empire deep into the Middle West. He fought with Gould again in the matter of the Chicago and Northwestern line. He bought scores of little short-line railroads and added them to his collection—but only when they abutted his New York Central system. He had no use for railroads for their own sake, but only for those railroads that added to his transportation empire.

William Henry Vanderbilt wanted to extend the Vanderbilt empire to the Pacific coast, but the Commodore wanted no part of that scheme. He had turned down a chance to get in on the Union Pacific Railroad, and had told the UP backers that they were crazy to get involved. But the fact probably was that Vanderbilt was growing old, and did not feel that either his son or any of his other executives could carry the responsibility of a trans-continental railroad.

Five years after he had acquired the Harlem Railroad, Vanderbilt was ready to consolidate all his lines, and finally the legislature allowed him to do so. New York Central stock, at the time of the consolidation, was worth more than $200 a share, and Hudson stock was worth $185. So although Vanderbilt had watered the stocks of his railroads time and again, still the public felt secure enough in their intrinsic value to keep the price of the stock far above any level it had ever reached before Vanderbilt took control.

By 1870, Commodore Vanderbilt was a legend in America. He was the owner of a vast industrial enterprise. After he acquired the Lake Shore railway his holdings were the most extensive in the nation. He was making efforts in these years to control the Western Union Telegraph Company. He owned a portion of the New York Municipal Gas Company and part of the Wagner Sleeping Car Company. He began to lay plans for the Grand Central terminal at Forty-second Street and Park Avenue in New York City, and he built a magnificent new freight depot at St. John's Park in lower Manhattan Island.

One day in the fall of 1869 Vanderbilt dedicated the new freight yard, which included an $800,000 bronze memorial in honor of the Commodore. President Ulysses S. Grant was invited to make the address of the day, but he said he could not come to New York at that time, so the mayor, Oakey Hall, was the speaker. A thousand men and women gathered to unveil the monument and hear Commodore Vanderbilt praised. Jay Gould, Jim Fisk, and scores of his other business enemies stood by and watched. Twenty-four sailors from the USS *Tallahassee* stood at attention while the band played and the speeches were made. Finally the cord was pulled, and the great bronze was unmasked for the public to see. It was one hundred fifty feet long and thirty-one feet high. It covered 3125 square feet and weighed fifty tons. It included copies of steamboats and railroad trains, forests, anchors, harbor scows—everything that had been important in Commodore Vanderbilt's past. On top of it all stood a colossal figure of Commodore Vanderbilt himself, in his white stock and heavy fur-trimmed overcoat. It was the most impressive display in all New York in its time, as was only proper. When the St. John's Park station was finally torn down, the statue was moved to the foot of the automobile ramp on the south side of Grand Central terminal, where Commodore Vanderbilt in his handsome overcoat looks over the city of New York to this day.

~ 10 ~

THE COMMODORE'S
GOLDEN YEARS

IN THE SUMMER of 1868 Commodore Vanderbilt went to
Saratoga Springs for his summer holiday. He went every
year to escape the heat and dullness of New York City
in July and August.

Most businessmen left New York in the summer
months and spent their time either at Saratoga, at Bar
Harbor, on Long Island, or at the new and developing
spa of Newport, Rhode Island. Several of Vanderbilt's
children liked to go to Newport, although he never
developed any fondness for that particular resort. He
liked Saratoga because it was cooler than New York, of
course, but also because many of his business acquaintances went there, and he found it easy to get up a game
of whist in the afternoons. Also he was addicted to harness
racing of trotting horses, and Saratoga Springs then
boasted the finest track and finest races in the area.

Vanderbilt had been traveling to Saratoga every
summer since 1840. For many years he stayed at the old
fashioned United States Hotel and kept a special suite
there. He became so prominent that the proprietor had
a clubhouse built in back of the hotel for Vanderbilt and
a handful of other guests. It was a kind of private club
where they used to retire in the afternoons to drink and
play cards in peace.

The Commodore got up early in the morning when he was at Saratoga. He would go down to the big dining room for breakfast. There he usually ate two lamb chops and the yolks of a couple of hardboiled eggs, then retired to the long front porch of the hotel to sit in a heavy wooden chair and enjoy a bit of conversation and an early cigar.

Perhaps he would take a walk in the morning, through the village or to the race track to talk to the grooms and inspect the trotters as they neighed and munched hay in their stalls. A half an hour at the exercise track, watching the racers go through their paces might then give way to an hour or two at whist in the clubhouse behind the hotel. Vanderbilt played there with eminently respectable company. Joseph Harper, the publisher, was one of his frequent whist partners. He also played with Chester W. Chapin, another railroad president, and when William Henry Vanderbilt had proved himself a good railroad man, he was allowed to come into the select group, too.

William Henry was in his father's confidence now. It was strange that it had taken the son forty years to win his father's respect, but he had done so by the manner in which he handled the bankrupt Staten Island Railroad. After Vanderbilt took over the Harlem Railroad, William Henry became a vice-president of that line. And when the Hudson and the Central were added, William Henry became his father's chief operating executive of all the roads. That did not mean that William Henry ran the railroads while the Commodore took his ease. Quite the contrary, as long as he lived the old man dominated his railroads, and no important decisions were made without his sanction.

The Commodore was the one who decided that the

new railroad station would be built at Forty-second Street
and Park Avenue. Others in his company believed that
spot was way too far uptown ever to be of any practical
use. They wanted the station placed somewhere around
Twenty-third Street, or certainly no further north than
Thirty-fourth Street. Vanderbilt's good judgment stood
the test of time: nearly a hundred years after his death
the location of the railroad station, in the heart of Manhattan Island, made it the best planned and best placed
railroad terminal in the world.

Vanderbilt also inaugurated several practices in railroading which persisted long after his death. Among
them was the practice of selling tickets in the railroad
station instead of on the trains. Until Vanderbilt's time
all passengers bought their tickets from the conductor,
after they had gotten on the train. But investigating that
practice, Vanderbilt learned that his conductors were
cheating the railroad, year after year. One of them, he
learned had saved more than $300,000 and owned a great
amount of real estate, although his salary was $1,000 a
year.

One of the ways in which the Commodore kept track
of the way his railroads were run was to ride in them
himself, and not always in the private car that could be
attached to the end of any train. When the Commodore
rode on the New York Central, whether in the private
car or not, he spent a good part of the trip marching
back and forth through the cars, examining them and
looking over the passengers and the way the conductors
and other railroad men went about their business.

At Saratoga, too, the Commodore spent at least part of
every day doing business. He read over the mail—at least
those letters his private secretary in New York felt like
sending on to him. He signed a few checks or notes in the

spidery scrawl he always used. He talked over problems of the day with William Henry, who managed to keep in very close touch with operations, and he made the decisions that had to be made. Then he turned his mind from work to pleasure.

Of all his recreations, the Commodore got the most pleasure from his trotting horses. Since the earliest days on Staten Island, he had loved fast horses. He had always kept a team, at least, in the stables behind the house. at 10 Washington Place. In New York, he drove up the island to race in the open country of the Bronx with other trotting enthusiasts. When he went to Staten Island to look over property, or to visit his brother Jake or one of his sisters, the Commodore always drove himself. One day, in fact, he drove himself so hard he nearly killed himself and Brother Jake as well.

Jake was out driving that day, going at a leisurely pace up the road, when he heard the thunder of hooves behind him. He did not turn around, but simply increased his own pace a bit, since no driver liked to be passed on the road. Not far ahead stood a narrow wooden bridge with high sides. It might be wide enough for two traps or even phaetons to pass, but it did not look wide enough. Jake determined that he would be first, no matter who this unknown was who was pelting along behind him. So Jake clucked at his horses, snapped the reins, and shouted as the team picked up speed. Still the thunder came on from behind, closer it seemed. Jake brought out his light whip and snapped it. The horses responded with a jolt, and the team sped toward the bridge. Finally, a few feet away, when it seemed impossible that a team could pass and still cross the bridge, a carriage whipped past Jake's rig, sideswiping him, and knocking his vehicle into the end of the bridge.

With a crash, Jake's phaeton smashed into the post, the front wheel was torn off, the traces ripped, and the startled team reared and whinnied in fright. The impact was so harsh that Jake was half thrown from his seat. Before he could get his balance, he heard the booming laugh of his brother, the Commodore, who stopped and came back to see that Jake was all right.

"You ought not try to beat your elder brother, Jake," the Commodore admonished him with a grin. And that day the two of them rode home to Jake's house on the hill, talking over old times as Jake's team plodded along behind them, the wrecked carriage left for servants to pick up and try to mend.

The Commodore's love for fast horses was so great that he kept a standing offer of $10,000 for a horse that could beat his own. Mountain Girl and Mountain Boy were a pair of favorites. The latter could do a mile in 2.06, and Vanderbilt was quite capable of driving him just that fast. One day, in fact, the Commodore took a friend out driving on the speedway that ran from Central Park up across Macomb's Dam Bridge and to Jerome Avenue in the Bronx. Vanderbilt drove along slowly enough, paralleling the Harlem Railroad tracks, until suddenly, just before they reached a crossing, he saw an express train bearing down on them. The Commodore felt an itch, and it was irresistible.

"Giddap," he shouted to the sleek pair of racers before him.

Like the thoroughbreds they were, the horses started immediately, and soon had the driving wagon pelting along at its best speed—too fast now to make the stop before the railroad tracks as any sane driver would have done.

The train whistled and hooted and black smoke

belched from her stack. The engineer leaned far out of his cab to crane his neck at the crazy man who was racing toward certain destruction.

Vanderbilt shouted at his team. The train sped on. The Commodore gave the reins a last desperate flick. The team and carriage jolted across the rails a few feet ahead of the whistling locomotive, and Vanderbilt, at his airiest, turned to wave at the white face of the frightened fireman in the cab above. Vanderbilt's passenger sat quiet, stunned.

"There is not another man in New York who could do that," the Commodore said proudly.

"And you will never do it again with me in your wagon," the frightened businessman replied.

At Saratoga, in that summer of 1868, Vanderbilt still took such chances, and still raced as hard as ever. His habits were such that for the past few years Saratoga had begun to bore his wife Sophia. She did not enjoy herself when left alone, or in the company of ladies of fashion, while the Commodore went off with the men to play cards or drive his horses. Sophia was a homebody. She much preferred to remain in her own home, surrounded by her daughters and grandchildren. There she felt at ease. In the alien atmosphere of Saratoga she felt old and tired.

So in 1868, Sophia did not accompany the Commodore to Saratoga. She did not want to stay in the emptiness of 10 Washington Place alone either, so she moved to the home of Horace Clark, the husband of her daughter Mary Louise. And there, on August 17, Sophia died at the age of 71.

When he heard the news, the Commodore ordered up a private train and one of his huge locomotives. Six hours later he was in New York City.

Sophia Vanderbilt was buried on August 19 in the old Moravian cemetery at New Dorp, on Staten Island. The cemetery and the church had a special significance to the Vanderbilt family. Old Jacob, the first Vanderbilt to settle on Staten Island, had helped to found the church. Since that time Vanderbilts had given labor and money to help it grow stronger in the community. The Commodore had built a small mausoleum in the cemetery, surmounted by a figure—Grief. Here he planned to be buried himself. Already he had sadly buried there the body of his favorite son, George Washington. Now a funeral procession left Manhattan Island on the Staten Island ferry and made its way slowly up the hill of the island to the church and cemetery. Alexander Turney Stewart, New York's most famous merchant, was a pall bearer for Mrs. Vanderbilt's last ceremony. So was Horace Greeley, editor of the *Tribune* and her dear friend and the friend of Cornelius Jeremiah Vanderbilt.

Sophia's death seemed to have little effect on the Commodore. It did not slow him down. Sometimes he seemed more vigorous than ever. He continued to acquire and consolidate railroads, and he continued to live a vigorous social life.

Into the Commodore's sphere at this time came a pair of female adventurers who were destined to become famous in American history. They were Victoria Claflin Woodhull and her sister Tennessee Claflin. Vanderbilt took a liking to them when he was first introduced to them by their father, Buck Claflin. Claflin had heard that the Commodore believed in spiritualism, and his girls were practicing spiritualists in those times. Later, Commodore Vanderbilt helped the sisters establish a brokerage house on Wall Street and a newspaper, called *Woodhull and Claflin's Weekly,* which was dedicated to

the cause of women's suffrage in those years before women had the right to vote or many other rights that were
equal to those of men.

Vanderbilt once proposed marriage to Tennessee
Claflin, but William Henry and his daughters objected
so seriously that the Commodore gave in to them. He
was determined, however, to take another wife. He was
too old to change his ways and move out of the house at
10 Washington Place, and he was not going to become
a lonely old man who sat and brooded in the silence of
a vacant mansion.

In the fall of 1868, just a few weeks after the death of
Sophia, Vanderbilt received a visit from two female
relatives whom he had never seen before. The Commodore's mother had a brother named Samuel Hand, who
had fought in the Revolutionary War on the side of the
colonists and had moved to Alabama afterward. The
ladies who came to New York were the granddaughter
and great-granddaughter of Samuel Hand. The Commodore was immensely pleased to see them, for he adored
his mother and in his visits to the spiritualists was constantly trying to get in touch with her in the other world.
He showed the ladies around New York, took them to
dinner at Delmonico's famous restaurant and made their
trip north as pleasant as possible. Samuel Hand's granddaughter, Mrs. Crawford, was a widow in her fifties.
Vanderbilt's friends and children thought it would make
a good match, since the Commodore was still a very spry
seventy-four years old.

But the Commodore had far younger ideas than any
of his contemporaries. He cast his eye on Samuel Hand's
great-granddaughter, Miss Frank Crawford, who was
thirty years old, and this is the lady he wooed during that
fall of 1868. He sent flowers and carriages to her door.

He sent her boxes of candy. He took her driving, with her mother, of course, through Central Park and up to Cato's roadhouse in the Bronx for dinner on Sundays. Finally, when the Crawfords found it time to return to Mobile in the fall, he sent Frank an autographed picture and asked her to write to him during the winter.

Frank Crawford and her mother returned to New York the following summer, as the Commodore had asked them to do. He lost no time then, in asking Frank to marry him. She accepted, for although he was nearly half a century older than she, Frank said she found him the most exciting man she had ever met.

Frank had only one request, that they be married by her family pastor, Dr. Charles F. Deems. But Dr. Deems could not leave Mobile at that moment, apparently, so the Commodore ordered a special train, and the two eloped to New London, Ontario, where they were married by a young minister.

It was scarcely a secret, although it was called an elopement. Frank and the Commodore got aboard their special train quietly enough but by the time it began picking up speed, all the countryside seemed to know about the affair, and all along their route the stations were jammed with people who had come out just to see the fabulous Commodore Vanderbilt and the young woman he had chosen to marry.

They spent their honeymoon at Saratoga. Frank enjoyed every minute of it, for unlike Sophia she loved riding in fast carriages, and she had so much influence on the Commodore that she persuaded him to give up his daily games of whist and five point euchre. When they returned to New York City in the fall, she even persuaded him to resign from half his social clubs and spend more time at home.

But while he did spend more time with his new wife than he had ever spent with the poor, uneducated Sophia, the Commodore did not stop tending to business. One of his finest moments, as a financier, came during the gold panic of 1869, which rose after Jim Fisk and Jay Gould had sought to corner the gold market. The gold cornering was stopped by a decision of President U. S. Grant to sell gold to the public at the current price. When Grant made that decision, the price of gold on Wall Street dropped from 160 to 138, and a number of speculators were ruined immediately. Even worse, however, was the general condition of the stock market, which responded to any such attempt immediately and with great exaggeration. Nearly all stocks fell—some of them thirty and forty points—which meant that speculators who bought on margin were in danger of losing their fortunes.

Commodore Vanderbilt saved the day in a way—not so much because of generosity but because he took that occasion, after New York Central stock had fallen several points, to buy heavily in his own stock. This increased his fortunes, of course, but it also brought a feeling of confidence and stability to Wall Street and helped prevent the gold panic from becoming a general panic.

General panic came four years later, in 1873. This violent upheaval was caused basically by speculation in railroad stocks over the years since the end of the Civil War. In the middle of the nineteenth century there was virtually no control at all over the practices of capitalists. Industrialists and businessmen did very much as they pleased, and while their speculations were injurious to the nation, still the immense growth of industry made it possible for a handful of men in New York and other big cities to speculate wildly, to win and lose fortunes, but yet not to slow the healthy growth of the nation. The reason was that railroads were needed. Transcontinental railroads in particular were so valuable that no matter how mismanaged their financial affairs might be, the people at large *had to use railroads* to ship their goods across the nation.

The entire year of 1873 was a shaky year. For the Commodore, personal involvement in tragedy began early in the year when the brokerage firm of Barton and Allen failed after a series of unwise speculations in rail stocks. Vanderbilt had risen above speculation by this time in his career, and he gave a great deal of business to that firm, because young Allen was his grandson. But when he heard that the firm was about to go bankrupt because of speculation, the Commodore hardened his heart. He clamped his teeth on his cigar and refused to save the firm. The boys had disobeyed his instructions. They would have to fend for themselves.

A few months later, hundreds of financial men in Wall Street faced the same dismal future. On September 18, Jay Cooke and Company closed its doors in Philadelphia. Other houses began to fail, for the Wall Street firms were closely connected in many cases, and many of them dealt in the same stocks that had caused the fall of Cooke.

The Commodore was out driving a pair of his trotters in Central Park when the panic struck Wall Street. For several years he had followed an invariable rule. He went to his downtown office early in the morning after breakfast, and there he attended to his stocks and general business affairs. About eleven o'clock he drove uptown to the offices of the New York Central, and there he spent two hours on railroad business, conferring with his son and with Chauncey Depew, a lawyer whom he had brought into railroading several years before. At one o'clock Vanderbilt's office day had ended. He went home for lunch, and then spent the afternoon out driving in one of his rigs.

The Commodore returned to Washington Place on this summer evening at about seven o'clock, to find reporters gathered there waiting for him. They did not even wait until he had finished giving his grooms orders about the horses, but demanded to know if he had heard of the events on Wall Street.

He had not. Further, he said calmly, he refused to comment on any aspect of financial affairs until he had gone into the house, eaten his dinner, and then looked over the evening paper. The reporters scurried back to their newspapers and out again to find other financial leaders willing to talk for publication. Vanderbilt settled back quietly to assess the situation.

He found it serious enough within the next few days that he conferred with President Grant, the Secretary of the Treasury, and other government officials who had come to New York, the nation's financial center. Vanderbilt had a scheme—even if many believed it was an outrageous one. He would offer $10,000,000 in securities of the New York Central Railroad if the government would put up $30,000,000 in bonds to stop the panic. President Grant did not accept the offer.

Vanderbilt did not behave very well, otherwise, during the panic. He owed the Union Trust Company $1,750,-000 on a call loan—which meant the bank should be able to get its money when it needed it. The bank did need the money during the panic, because frightened speculators were withdrawing all they had to cover losses, or to be sure they got their cash before something happened to the bank. But Vanderbilt would not pay. He said, later, that he could not pay. Whatever the truth of that, the

Union Trust Company went bankrupt before Vanderbilt did pay the notes, and he did not pay them until the
federal government had quieted the panic by buying
back for gold $20,000,000 in government bonds.

The Commodore's reputation, gained in the previous
gold panic of 1869, vanished overnight, and in 1873 he
became a favorite target of the newspapers, along with
Jay Gould. They recalled, now, how Vanderbilt had mis-
used the public confidence in the way he ran his steamship lines. They recalled the danger of traveling aboard
Vanderbilt trains in the early days.

But newspaper talk did not upset the Commodore.
While the journalists complained about him, Vanderbilt
set out to have his own way again by conducting rate
wars with the Pennsylvania Railroad, the Baltimore and
Ohio, and of course with his old enemies of the Erie.
And then, when the rate wars began to pinch everyone,
he forced the other railroads to join him in an eastern
railroad alliance, which was, in many ways, the greatest
trust of its time. By the time he was eighty years old,
Vanderbilt was a legend.

~ 11 ~

THE LAST DAYS OF A
RAILROAD BARON

AT EIGHTY, the Commodore seemed uncommonly healthy
and active. He had already outlived nearly all his peers.
Old John Jacob Astor died in 1848, and his son William
Backhouse Astor died in 1875. A. T. Stewart died in
1876. But the Commodore lived on, competing and ar-
guing with far younger men.

In May, 1876, for the first time, he began to show the
signs of age, however. He was sent to bed with a severe
intestinal infection which kept him confined for months.
He hoped to be up and around again. In the beginning
he was asking Dr. Linsly when he might be able to drive
again in Central Park. But almost from the beginning of
this illness, Dr. Linsly and the rest of the family knew
that the Commodore was nearing the end of his life. To
Linsly and others it was something of a marvel that the
Commodore had lasted so long on his feet. Thirty years
before the Commodore had suffered heart palpitations
so severe that some believed he would die then. He had
kidney inflammations and other disorders through the
years. But the Commodore's will power was too great for
any of these diseases until now.

The Commodore's illness lasted all spring and summer and drifted on into the fall. William Henry spent

the summer of 1876 at Saratoga, as he had done for so long, but the Commodore could not be moved, and so Frank did not leave either. She and her mother kept vigil in the big house on Washington Place, through the torrid days of July and August.

In the fall, even the Commodore began to realize that his end was near. He had revised his will a number of times in recent years, mostly to add charitable bequests and to remember friends and relatives. But now, knowing that he had not many more months to live, the Commodore sought to assure the continuation of his lines and the valuable empire he had created in the New York Central Railroad.

The Commodore was not much interested in the dividends that the railroad paid, or in the amounts of money that could be made in other stocks. Now he realized that control of their railroad was the key to the future. He knew that the nation was growing, as it had grown each year of his long and fruitful life. He knew that as the nation grew New York City would grow even more important than it was by 1875, and that the riches of the whole area depended in good part on the transportation system. He knew that control of the Central would give the family an important place in the affairs of the nation.

Unfortunately the Commodore had not ever communicated very well with his immediate family. William Henry, who now stood second in command only to the Commodore himself, did not understand his father, and said so, bluntly. He had grown up in quite a different tradition, because when William Henry's health failed him in those early years in Wall Street, the boy had gone to make his life on the Staten Island farm.

Vanderbilt had helped his son then only by buying a farm with a ramshackle house and a lean-to kitchen. In the twenty years that William Henry spent as a farmer, he received very little financial help and much abuse from his father. The Commodore, of course, could not stand physical weaklings around him. Nor did he have any respect for farmers, because he had hated farm life so much himself. So father and son grew apart in the important early years and remained that way. Even when William Henry had proved his abilities in operating the Staten Island rail line, they did not grow much closer together personally.

William Henry tried to please his father. He took up racing trotters, and he bought a box coach which he painted in maroon and white—later to be the Vanderbilt family colors. William Henry also proved to be the only real friend to Frank Vanderbilt in the family—which the Commodore noted and appreciated.

Most important of all, William Henry proved to his father's satisfaction that he could run railroads very well. The younger Vanderbilt had learned accounting in his early days. He brought that kind of detailed mind to railroad operation, and while perhaps he was not as acute as the Commodore in sensing opportunity, he was a good businessman. The problem was that William Henry had not built up the railroad empire from a small beginning himself, and as time passed, William Henry began to have more regard for the fortune that the family had amassed than he had for the properties that brought the fortune.

The Commodore once told one of his attorneys that all a man really needed from life was a million dollars. That was as much as he could spend, and that was as much as anyone ought to have.

"Well, Commodore," said the lawyer, "there is a very easy way of getting rid of the rest."

"No, there ain't," the old man replied in his own strong but ungrammatical way. "For what you have got isn't worth anything, unless you have got the power, and if you give away the surplus, you give away the control."

There, in a sentence, was Commodore Vanderbilt's philosophy of business. It was not shared by William Henry Vanderbilt, and for good reason. In this period in American history, bankers began to play a far more important part in business life than ever before. Among the bankers, the leading figure was to become J. Pierpont Morgan, a young man whose father had emigrated to England to establish a banking firm in what was then the financial capital of the world.

J. P. Morgan was a convincing man. It was to the advantage of bankers to spread the investment in American industry into the hands of many people. Thus the bankers would have a share, and would be able to handle more business in more ways. So Morgan began to convince various businessmen that they would be better off spreading control of their enterprises widely. That way these men felt they could retain control of their businesses with small minority interests in stock. The system seemed well-planned. William Henry Vanderbilt was convinced that it would work out well, and he was also convinced that it was wise to spread around investments, so that the basic fortune would be protected.

William Henry did not know, in 1876, the exact content of his father's will. Yet there was a great amount of money to go around among all the children, he did know that.

The Commodore was not so sure. He was concerned lest the control of the Vanderbilt empire be lost. He did not trust his daughters or his son Cornelius Jeremiah, because he felt they had no feeling for the railroads. He was afraid that if he gave one daughter three million dollars and another five million dollars, they would first turn William Henry out of the presidency of the railroads, and would then begin squabbling among themselves. Six months later, he felt, they would begin to lose everything.

The important matter to the Commodore now was not money, but a place in history for himself and his family. He wanted desperately to make of the New York Central Railroad a monument to the Vanderbilts.

With that in mind, the Commodore roused himself from his sick bed in the fall of 1876 and changed his will once again. This time, he said, he had taken care that the stock of the railroad would be secured in such a way that it could not be put on the market after he was dead.

Having done that, he relaxed.

In the fall, the daughters learned that the Commodore had changed his will, and one by one they came to discover what they could about the changes. Ethelinda, Emily, Eliza, and Sophia came. So did Mary Alicia and Mary Louise. Catherine Juliet had married a Frenchman and she lived across the Atlantic. Frances, the sickly one of the family, had died unmarried.

But the others came. They argued and they lost their tempers. Some of them called Frank names. The Commodore heard of their insults and lost his temper too. But all this family argument settled nothing, and changed nothing, for the Commodore had taken his action on the basis of principle. He knew the girls would not like what he had done. He was concerned mostly that the lawyers had drawn the will properly so it would stand in court.

Cornelius Jeremiah came to visit his father, too. He was a pitiful figure, shorter than the Commodore, wearing a dark beard and mustache. He pleaded for an opportunity to work on the railroads, but neither his father nor William Henry believed that the gambling instinct could serve the New York Central well. Cornelius Jeremiah claimed that he had reformed. William Henry had him followed by a private detective, who reported that Cornelius Jeremiah went into one gambling house after another. In the end, the Commodore washed his hands of his younger son and refused to see him again.

When the Commodore had fallen ill, the New York newspapers reported that he was dead. One or another of the newspapers had been reporting that fact for ten years, but every time it happened, it caused a flurry of excitement in Wall Street. No other man had so much importance there. For years Vanderbilt had been known as The Great Cornerer, following his twin successes in cornering the stock of the Harlem Railroad and outfoxing Daniel Drew. It was well known that the Commodore preached against speculation these days, but no one in Wall Street knew whether or not he truly followed his own advice. So each time the death report came out, the stocks in which the Commodore was known to have interested himself began to rise and fall erratically.

By late fall, 1876, it was apparent to the press that the Commodore was on his death bed. How long he might last was anybody's guess. But the facts indicated that he would never rise again from his couch and go to the office. Dr. Linsly spent most of his time at the Vanderbilt mansion. A half dozen specialists came in and out. Nurses were employed both day and night. Everything possible was being done for the old Commodore—everything that money could buy. But no one could arrest the progress of old age and disease.

In his last months the Commodore lived in almost constant pain. The nurses gave him laudanum to quiet his nerves and tried to get him to drink beef tea, which he spit all over the bed. He liked soothing music, so Mrs. Crawford played hymns for him on a portable organ that was brought into the house.

At first he remained in bed in his own bedroom, but later they brought him down from the third floor to the second floor, so he could be better managed and could listen to the music. Frank often sang for him in the evenings, and both Frank and her mother were on constant call during his bad spells. Sometimes he would rouse them out at three o'clock in the morning to play hymns and sing to him.

The death reports continued. One day a pair of reporters came to the door to ask if the Commodore was dead. He heard them talking to the maid.

"It's a damned lie," he shouted down the stairs.

The reporters knew that voice. They went back to their newspapers, smiling. The old Commodore was still alive, they assured their editors.

Finally, on January 4, 1877, the Commodore felt sure that the end was coming, and he asked Dr. Linsly to call the family together for one last meeting. At ten o'clock that morning thirty of his relatives came to the sickroom, to say goodby to the old patriarch who had managed the family's affairs for so many years. Dr. Linsly and the specialists were there. So was Frank's Dr. Deems, for Vanderbilt had brought Dr. Deems to New York and given him a church on Mercer Street to please his wife. Further, in this last illness, the Commodore had seized upon Christianity after having ignored it largely for most of the years of his life.

There was nothing to be done. The Commodore's constant bladder infection had finally ruptured and peritonitis had developed. His entire abdominal cavity was affected.

As the family gathered, the Commodore grew progressively weaker. His sturdy frame had weakened in the long illness, as fever wasted the muscles and swept the weight from him. Yet even in these last hours he was an impressive figure, with snow white mane of hair and white side burns that concealed the shriveling of his cheeks.

One after another, William Henry and the other children stepped forward to speak a last word to their father. The Commodore had conducted his last serious conversation with William Henry days before, warning him that he would be entrusted to carry out the terms of the will and asked him to do it faithfully. In that last talk, too, the Commodore had asked William Henry to enlarge the mausoleum on Staten Island, and to make of it a traditional last home for the remains of all the male Vanderbilts and their wives. The girls would not be buried there. They would follow their husbands to other graves. But Vanderbilts, the males of the line and their mothers, would rest in the family vault.

William Henry had promised to honor all these requests. This final meeting, on January 4, was simply to say farewell.

The Commodore asked that someone sing, and Mrs. Crawford sang one of his favorite hymns—then another. He brightened and smiled, and tried to speak but choked. The doctor cleared his throat and propped him up. He gestured weakly and smiled again.

"That was a good prayer," he said, when Dr. Deems finished the Lord's Prayer.

At ten-thirty, he closed his eyes for a moment and stopped trying to communicate. He opened his eyes again, but said nothing more. A few minutes later, he seemed to have gone. One of the physicians said there was no sight in the eyes. Vanderbilt heard, raised one hand, and closed his eyelids. A few moments later he drew one long, rasping breath and died. The king of American railroads had breathed his last.

EPILOGUE

FROM THE DAY of the Commodore's death, the fortunes of the Vanderbilt family did not prosper. The Commodore left a total of more than a hundred million dollars in his estate. He was the richest man in America. He left more money than there was in the United States treasury on the day of his death. In terms of what he controlled and how much it grew to be worth, he was the richest man in the world. Only the Duke of Westminster in England had nearly as much, and his fortune was in land, not in an industrial empire that was to grow with the nation. Almost all of the Commodore's fortune was left to William Henry Vanderbilt, as custodian for his children and for generations yet unborn. The Commodore's intent had been to keep the railroad in the hands of Vanderbilt men for all time.

William Henry did not heed his father's wishes. The story of the dissolution of the Vanderbilt empire is another story in itself. But in the end, after three more generations, control of the New York Central Railroad passed out of Vanderbilt hands entirely and into those of strangers.

In later years, the Commodore was attacked and reviled as one of the evil "robber barons" who dominated

159

America in the period between 1865 and the beginning of the twentieth century. The attacks on the Commodore and others did not take into account the manner of the times, and the way in which even the United States federal government looked upon money and financial affairs. In those days, particularly before the coming of Teddy Roosevelt to political life, in business it was every man for himself. There was no general concept of "public responsibility." The major precept of business was *caveat emptor*—let the buyer beware. More, the business and industrial communities operated on a basis of complete selfishness and mistrust. Public works and public utilities existed, the business men thought, for the purpose of private profit.

It was many years before this concept changed in American life, although the anti-trust laws and some effective railroad regulation began shortly after the Commodore's death. But to condemn Commodore Vanderbilt for ruthlessness and inhumanity is the same as to ask that Charlemagne or Henry VIII be brought to answer for their actions on the level of contemporary society. Commodore Vanderbilt was a man of his own times, which encompassed the days of George Washington, of Abraham Lincoln, even of Rutherford B. Hayes, when effective political and business reform was just beginning in America. Vanderbilt was a business genius and a man as strong and pithy as the buccaneers he often seemed to imitate in his methods. Those methods might not seem admirable in the last half of the twentieth century, and yet forgetting all method, the character remains. It was strength that made Cornelius Vanderbuilt a commodore of the greatest merchant fleet in America, and then the mogul of a monstrous railroad empire. In the end it was character, nothing more nor less than that.

BIBLIOGRAPHY

ANDREWS, WAYNE. *The Vanderbilt Legend.* New York: Harcourt, Brace, and Co., 1941.

BAYLES, RICHARD M. *History of Richmond County.* New York: L. E. Preston and Co., 1887.

CHOULES. JOHN OVERTON. *The Cruise of the Steam Yacht North Star.* Boston: Gould and Lincoln, 1854.

CLUTE, J. J. *Annals of Staten Island.* New York: New York Press of Charles Vogt, 1877.

CROFFUT, W. A. *The Vanderbilts.* New York: Belford, Clarke and Co., 1886.

CROWNINSHIELD, FRANK. "House of Vanderbilt." *Vogue,* (New York), November 15, 1941. (Magazine article.)

FISKE, STEPHEN. *Off-hand Portraits of Prominent New Yorkers.* New York: George R. Lockwood and Son, 1884.

FLYNN, JOHN T. *Men of Wealth.* New York: Simon and Schuster, 1941.

HART, SMITH. *The New Yorkers.* New York: Sheridan House, 1938.

HOLBROOK, STEWART H. *Age of the Moguls.* New York: Doubleday, 1953.

In Memorium Cornelius Vanderbilt. Vanderbilt University, 1877.

JOSEPHSON, MATTHEW. *The Robber Barons.* New York: Harcourt, Brace, and Co., 1934.

LANE, WHEATON J. *Commodore Vanderbilt.* New York: Alfred A. Knopf, 1942.

LANG, C. W., and DAVIS, W. T. *Staten Island and Its People: A History, 1609-1929.* New York: Lewis Historical Publishing Co., 1930.

McADAM, ROGER WILLIAMS. *Salts of the Sound.* New York: Stephen Daye Press, 1939.

MARSHALL, DAVID. *Grand Central.* New York: Whittlesay House, 1946.

Memorial of the Golden Wedding of Cornelius and Sophia Vanderbilt. Privately printed. New York, 1864.

METZMAN, GUSTAV. *Commodore Vanderbilt (1794-1877), Forefather of the New York Central.* New York: The Newcomen Society of England, American Branch, 1946.

MINNIGERODE, MEADE. *Certain Rich Men.* New York: G. P. Putnam's Sons, 1927.

MORRIS, IRA K. *Morris' Memorial History of Staten Island.* New York: Memorial Publishing Co., 1898.

MYERS, GUSTAVUS. *History of the Great American Fortunes.* New York: Charles H. Kerr Co., 1911.

PARTON, JAMES. *Famous Americans of Recent Times.* Boston: Houghton, Mifflin Co., 1884.

SMALES, HOLBERT T. *The Breakers.* Newport, R.I.: Remington Ward, 1952.

SMITH, MATTHEW H. *Sunshine and Shadow in New York.* Hartford: Burr & Hyde, 1868.

INDEX